BAKERY INGREDIENTS AND TOOLS

DR ANSHUMALI PANDEY

Contents

Preface

In an increasingly globalized world and the changing paradigm of urbanized living the demand for Hospitality and Tourism has increased manifold the world over. In this ever expanding sector, it has become essential to provide Competency based Vocational Education. It is in this context this book on Bakery attempts, to describe in detail about the Ingredients and Tools necessary for the Bakery Business.

The language used in this book is simple without any pictorial illustration to keep the cost low and affordable to all. This book is a complete handbook for anybody to even start a small bakery. This book will help students by giving them information in simple story telling style. The Author of the book is a practicing professional from the fields of Hospitality and Tourism and has an experience of over 25 years.

I hope this book will serve a useful resource in this subject. Comments and Suggestions are welcome for further improvement of the Book.

Best Wishes

Dr Anshumali Pandey

Preface

In an increasingly globalized world and the changing paradigm of [illegible] demand for Hospitality and Tourism [illegible] world over [illegible] ever expanding sector, it has become essential to [illegible] Competency Based [illegible] Education. It is in this context this book on Bakery [illegible] about [illegible] Bakery [illegible]

[illegible]

[illegible]

Prologue

Baking is the cooking of food by dry heat in an oven in which the action of the dry convection heat is modified by steam. The dry heat of baking changes the form of starches in the food and causes its outer surfaces to brown, giving it an attractive appearance and taste. The browning is caused by caramelization of sugars. When baking, consideration must be given to the amount of fat that is contained in the food item. Higher levels of fat such as margarine, butter or vegetable shortening will cause an item to spread out during the baking process. A bakery (or baker's shop) is an establishment which produces and sells flour-based food baked in an oven such as bread, cakes, pastries and pies.

CHAPTER I

Bakery Ingredients and Tools: Introduction.

Bakery ingredients have been used since ancient times and are of utmost importance these days as perhaps nothing can be baked without them. They are available in wide varieties and their preferences may vary according to the regional demands. Easy access of global information and exposure of various bakery products has increased the demand for bakery ingredients.

Baking ingredients offer several advantages such as reduced costs, volume enhancement, better texture, colour, and flavour enhancement. For example, ingredients such enzymes improve protein solubility and reduce bitterness in end products, making enzymes one of the most preferred ingredients in the baking industry.

> "*Every ingredient in a recipe has a specific purpose. It's also important to know how to mix or combine the ingredients properly, which is why baking is sometimes referred to as a science. There are reactions in baking that are critical to a recipe turning out correctly. Even some small amount of variation can dramatically change the result. Whether its breads or cake, each ingredient plays a part.*"

Food Ingredients– *The different ingredients used in baking are flour, refined flour or maida, sugar, shortenings, leavening agents, eggs, water, salt, milk and milk derivatives. The bakery ingredients can be classified depending upon their functions in bakery.*

Structure builders: *Provide the structure and texture to the bakery products e.g. flour, eggs and milk.*

Tenderizers*: Provide softness and shortness in the product e.g. fat, sugar and baking powder.*

Moisteners: *Provide moisture and keeping quality e.g. milk, water, egg, syrup. Driers: Absorb and retain moisture and provide the body of the product e.g. milk solids and starches.*

Flavors*: Provide natural flavour e.g. cocoa, chocolate, butter, egg, vanilla and other natural flavoring ingredients.*

CHAPTER II

SUGARS

Sugar or as it is chemically called Sucrose is a building blocks of carbohydrates and it is naturally found in many food such as fruit, milk, vegetables and grain, another kind of sugar is added sugar which can be founded in flavored yogurt, sweetened beverages, baked goods and cereals, and it is used widely in industry. Sugar is one of the major ingredients in the bakery industry and plays an important role. Sugars vary in their sweetening quality and are the soul of all desserts. Sugar is natural and non –toxic, sweet testing, water soluble concentrated form or crystalline carbohydrate.

A molecule of sugar is composed of 12 atoms of carbon, 22 atoms of hydrogen, and 11 atoms of oxygen (C12H22O11). There are two basic groups of sugars – simple sugars or monosaccharides, which means single sugars" like glucose and fructose, and complex sugars or disaccharides, meaning "double sugars" like maltose (malt sugar} and lactose (found in animal milk).

Origin:

It is found naturally and in higher quantity in the leaves, stems, roots or fruits of plants. Sugar may be obtained from varied plants like from maple tree – Canada, date palm – Africa, sugarcane – tropical region like India, beetroots from temperate region like Russia and from sorghum, grapes, potatoes, honey etc. The primary sugar, glucose, is a product of photosynthesis and occurs in all green plants.

In most plants, the sugars occur as a mixture that cannot readily be separated into the components. In the sap of some plants, the sugar mixtures are condensed into syrup. Juices of sugarcane (Saccharumofficinarum) and sugar beet (Beta vulgaris) are rich in pure sucrose, although beet sugar is generally much less sweet than cane sugar. These two sugar crops are the main sources of commercial sucrose.

Classification of Sugar :

Sugars are classified under one or in the combination of following –

1. The source (sugarcane or sugar beet)
2. The country of origin
3. The method of processing, which in turn determine the type of sugar produced, e.g. cube sugar, icing sugar.
4. Catering use – specific type of sugar should purchase for particular use. Chemical group –sugar may be classified in two chemical groups, mono and disaccharides.

Manufacture of sugar :

The first step in sugar production is to crush the cane or beet to extract the juice. This juice contains tannins, pigments, proteins and other undesirable components that must be removed through refinement with the help of chemicals (milk of lime or carbon dioxide). Refinement begins by dissolving the juice in water, then boiling it in large steam evaporators. The solution is then crystallized in heated vacuum pans. The un–crystallized liquid by –product, known as molasses, is separated out in a centrifuge (used mainly as cattle fodder). The remaining crystallized product, known as raw sugar, contains many

impurities. This is then washed with steam to remove some of the impurities. This yields a product known as turbinado sugar. Refining continues as the turbinado is heated, liquefied, centrifuged and filtered. Chemicals may be used to bleach and purify the liquid sugar. Finally, the clear liquid sugar is recrystallized in vacuum pans and further refined through bone ash to get pure opaque granulated sugar. Pure sucrose is sold in granulated
and powdered forms and is available in several grades.

Forms of Sugar:

1. **Granulated/ white sugar/sandy sugar** –This is the regular white sugar which in used in homes. Usage of this sugar will find its place in any preparation which has sufficient liquid to dissolve it. For example, whipping eggs, making sugar syrups, cooking sabayon over double boilers, etc. It contains 99.7% sucrose.

2. **Icing sugar** – Granulated sugar is crushed into fine powder and has a small percentage of corn starch added to keep it smooth and free flowing. Icing sugar is used for creaming methods where it would be used as icing for cakes and pastries. Icing sugar can also be sifted on top of dry baked sweet products as a garnish.

3. **Castor sugar** – This is superfine sugar (A Grade) and is also called breakfast sugar –made by crushing and sieving fine granulated sugar. It dissolves quickly and easily in liquids and can be creamed easily. Used in making pastries, cakes, desserts, ices etc. as it produce tender and light cakes.

4. **Pearl sugar** – is a type of decorating sugar made by polishing large crystals until they resemble pearls.

5. **Sugar cubes** – are formed by pressing moistened granulated sugar into molds and allowing it to dry. Most cubes are used for beverage service.

6. **Powder Sugar or confectioners' sugar** – It is obtained from granulated sugar by pulverization (refining of granulated sugar to get more fine form). It is available in various degree of fineness, use for different purposes in confectionary.

7. **Brown Sugar** – It is simple refined sugar with some molasses returned to it or it is the residual sugar obtained during the process of refining sugar. It is brown in color and has distinctive color and flavor. As it contains moisture, it forms lump. Used in the preparation of certain puddings, cakes, etc.The more darker coarse granulated and caramel flavor sugar is called Turbinado sugar in USA and Demirara sugar in Great Britain. It is used in beverages and certain baked products.

8. **Vergeoise sugar or Sucre vergeoise** (French) – solid residue from refining beet giving a product of soft consistency, golden or brown with pronounced color. Sucre vergeoise is available in blonde (light) or brune (dark).

9. **Muscovado sugar** – is an unrefined or partially refined cane sugar with a strong molasses flavor and high moisture content. It has a slightly coarse texture and feels sticky to the touch. It is popularly used in chocolate sweets and other baked goods. It is also called Barbados sugar, molasses sugar, kandasari, khand, and moist sugar.

10. **Glucose** – It is present in body and in fruits in natural form. Commercially it is sold as Dextrose. It is less sweet than sucrose, but it is use because of its waster holding capacity. It has ability to control the size of the crystals in candies and as a food for yeast, during the fermentation.

11. **Liquid glucose** – Liquid glucose is obtained by treating the corn slurry by acid – a process known as hydrolysis. This is chemically made and results in a thick viscous liquid that is used to produce candies by not allowing the sugar to crystallize and also acts as a preservative. Liquid glucose contains the dextrin gum which retards the crystallization of sugar. When added to products, it makes them pliable and hence very commonly used to prepare garnishes and decoration pieces with sugar.

12. **Fondant** – sugar syrup beaten with cream of tartar to form thick white paste. Used for decorating pastry or confectionary.

13. **Date sugar** – It is obtained from drying and pulverizing dates. It is very sweet and although it does not dissolve very well it is used in many baked products.

14. **Liquid caramel** – liquid sugar in which caramel colour is added to give it dark brown colour. It is a thick free –flowing liquid and may be used in preparation of puddings and some types of confectionary.

15. **Treacle/Molasses** – are products of refined sugar. When the sugarcane juice undergoes refining, it undergoes many stages. In the first stage the white sugar or the raw sugar is removed. The remaining sugar syrup is used to make treacle which is stronger than golden syrup but less than molasses. Used in the preparation of certain beverages and sauces.

16. **Maltose** – It is use as a flavoring and coloring agent in the brewing of beer.

17. **Lactose**– It is commercially extracted solution of whey formed by crystallization. It is usually added to bakery products because its presence adds to the brewing of food products.

18. **Isomalt** – It is a natural sugar substitute and in reality it is sugar alcohol. It is available in crystalline forms and is used for preparing sugar garnishes as it is more stable than sugar and does not caramelize thereby giving an appearance of thin glass sheets.

19. **Golden Syrups** – It is thick amber coloured liquid obtained from sugar during the refining process. It is treated with acid to cut down on the sharp taste. It looks similar to honey and is used in making confectionery products and to add flavour to the food products.

20. **Honey** –It is natural sugar consisting of glucose and fructose. It is a natural sugar obtained from bee hives. The colour and flavor of honey will vary with its source. Some commercial honey farms allow bees to suck the nectar from only one particular flower to produce the honey of that flavor. One can use honey in most of the baked products but care has to be taken as honey can caramelize even at lower temperatures. It is used as leavening agents and in sherbets.

21. **Maple syrup** – It is natural sweetener and is a sap of maple tree. It is boiled down to thick syrup. Pure maple syrup is very expensive, as to obtain 1 liter of maple one has to boil down at least 10 liters of maple sap. For easy processing, commercial maple syrup added to them. It could be added in the range of 2 –6 percent. The percentage of the maple is always mentioned on the bottle and this decides the price of the product.

22. **Palm sugar** – Palm sugar is traditionally made from the sap of Palmyra palm or the date palm. It is extensively used in Asian cooking.

23. **Agave syrup** is produced from starches extracted from. It has a neutral flavor about 25% sweeter than sugar, and a consistency that is thinner than honey. It may be used

in baking and cooking, as well as for sweetening beverages.

24. **Corn Syrup** – It is very sweet and contains high amount of fructose and glucose or dextrose. It is chemically refined clear syrup made from corn kernels and is prepared by converting corn starch into simple sugar compound by the use of enzymes. Coloured corn syrup is artificially coloured. Used in icing, candy masking and beverages.

25. **Invert sugar** –When a sucrose solution is heated with an acid, some of the sucrose breaks down into equal parts of two simple sugars, dextrose and levulose. A mixture of equal parts of dextrose and levulose is called. It is about 30% sweeter than regular sucrose. Invert sugar has two properties that make it interesting to the baker. First, it holds moisture especially well and, therefore, helps keep cakes fresh and moist. Second, it resists crystallization. Thus, it promotes smoothness in candies, icings, and syrups. This is why an acid such as cream of tartar is often added to sugar syrups. The acid inverts some of the sugar when it is boiled, thus preventing graininess in the candy or icing. Invert sugar is produced commercially. It is also present in honey. The use of invert sugar has declined since glucose syrup is cheaper and, for some uses, has superior properties. Some bakers and confectioners take the view that invert syrup improves the flavour of some products."Artificial honey" – Technically the same as inverted sugar syrup, the product is sometimes nicknamed artificial honey thanks to its honey –like flavor.

Artificial sugar:

These are nonnutritive sweeteners, or non –caloric sweeteners, are sweeteners that contain virtually no calories and no carbohydrate. These sweeteners are chemicals or plant –based substances that are hundreds of times sweeter than regular sugar (sucrose) and that have little or no effect on blood sugar levels. Sugar substitutes are very popular among people who have diabetes, as well as the general population.

<u>Some artificial sweeteners are –</u>

"• *Saccharine – 300 –500 times sweeter than sugar. It can replace some of the sugar, but will leave a metallic aftertaste and may result in lumpy texture.*

• *Aspartame – 200 times sweeter than sugar. Not for baking as it loses sweetness in high heat. May work in custards and puddings.*

• *Sucralose – 600 times sweeter than sugar and is heat stable. Good for baking under restricted baking formulation, which has low –calorie fillers added for bulk. Sucralose is a distant cousin of sugar as it is made from sugar.*

• *Acesulfame potassium, or Ace –K –200 times sweeter than sugar and is heat stable. Can be used in baking, but will yield a slight bitter aftertaste.*

• *Erythritol –150 times sweeter than sugar. Good for baking with no aftertaste; has fewer calories than sugar, but is not zero –calorie like many other artificial sweeteners.*

• *Stevia –200 to 300 times sweeter than sugar.Heat stable so can be used in baking; however, these sugars do not caramelize or crystallize so you will not get the browning effect desired in certain baked goods. Not appropriate for use in meringues.*

• *Neotame –8,000 times sweeter than sugar. Developed to be used in baking as the sweetness holds up to high heat with no metallic or bitter aftertaste.*"

Uses of Sugar –

• Adds sweetness and flavour to the products.

• To colour the cooked products by the process of Caramelization.

• They give crust color. And help get even texture.

• Makes the texture firm and tender by weakening the gluten strands.

• To retain moisture and prevent in particularly baked goods such as cakes from drying out.

• Act as preservative.

• To help as an activator, sugar helps yeast to grow faster by providing it with a readily available source of nourishment.

• As anti –coagulant.

• They act as creaming agents with fats and as foaming agents with eggs.

• As a main ingredient for cake decorating, e.g. different types of icing (topping the cake).

Cooking of Sugar –

1. One should take the following precautions while cooking sugar –
2. Use thick bottom bowl.
3. Equipment should be clean and free from oil grease.
4. Use quality sugar
5. Add sufficient water so that it will dissolve well.
6. Add lemon juice before the solution reaches boiling point
7. Lemon juice helps remove dust from sugar syrup
8. Use slow fire and do not stir the syrup when boiling.
9. Remove the scum with the help of a thick wet cloth.
10. During boiling, small specks of sugar crystals will be sprayed on ti. It must be removed.
11. Stop the boiling when the required stage has been reached.

12. If the sugar has gone over the required stage, adjust by adding warm water.

13. Maintain the correct temperature.

14. Follow the methods carefully.

15. If colour or essence is added, ensure that they are free from oil.

Making Sugar Syrups:

Simple or stock syrups are solutions of sugar and water. They are used in the bakeshop to moisten cakes and to make sauces, fruit sorbets, butter creams and candied fruits. The syrups density or concentration is dictated by its intended purpose. Cold water will dissolves up to double its weight in sugar, heating the solution forms denser, more concentrated syrups. A hydrometer, which measures specific gravity and shows degrees off concentration on Baume scale is the most accurate guide to density.

Simple syrups can be prepared without the aid of a hydrometer, however. To make simple sugar syrups, specific amounts of water and sugar combined in a saucepan and brought to a boil. Once the solution boils, it the important no to stir, as this may cause recrystallization or lumping. For making successful simple sugar syrups like –

• **Light syrups** – boil 2 parts water which 1 part sugar for one minute. This concentration would measure – 17 –20c on the Baume scale. Light syrups can be used for making sorbet or moistening sponge cake.

• **Medium syrup** – boil 1 part sugar with 1 – ½ part water for 1 minute. This concentration would measure 21 –24c on the Baume scale. Medium syrups can be used for candying citrus peel.

• **Heavy syrups** – boil equal part of water and sugar for 1 minute. This concentration would measure 28 –30c on the Baume scale, and the solution should be at 220f (104c) heavy syrups are a basic, all – purpose syrup kept on hand in many bakeshops.

Functional Properties of Sugar in food –

In addition to the main role of sugars in providing sweet taste, there many other functions of sugars in food.

• **Sweetness** – The most apparent sensory property of sugars such as glucose, fructose, and sucrose is their sweetness, Lactose (milk sugar) is the least sweet, whereas fructose is the sweetest sugar. Sugars areused assweeteners in many kindsof food products.

• **Preservation** – By absorbing free water and increasing osmotic pressure, sugar reduces water activity in a food system (e.g. jam), resulting in reduced microbial and mold growth as well as extending the storage life of food. Also sugar can preserve fruits, either in syrup with fruit such as apples, pears..... or in crystallized form where the preserved material is cooked in sugar to the point of crystallization and the resultant product is then stored dry. This method can be used for the skins of citrus fruit (candied peel), angelica and ginger. A modification of this process produces glace fruit such as glace cherries where the fruit is preserved in sugar but is then extracted from the syrup and sold, the sugar content of the fruit and the superficial coating of syrup maintain the preservation. Using of sugar is often combined with alcohol for preservation of luxury products such as fruit in brandy or other spirits.

• **Flavor** – Sugar plays an important and single role in contributing to the flavor of food by interacting with othercomponents to enhance or lessen certain flavors. By adding a small amount of sugar to cooked vegetables and meat enhance the food's natural flavors, without making them taste sweet. In sour applications such as beverages, jams and marmalades which all mixes of sweet and sour components, it is important to create a good balance between sourness and sweetness, which is often achieved by adding a mix of sugar and citric acid. In bitter applications, sugar is often used to moderate or disguise the bitterness (chocolate and coffee).

• **Antioxidant Function** – The hygroscopic nature of sugar produces a weakantioxidant effect by decreasing the availability of water that is otherwise required to potential oxidants. The antioxidanteffect of sugar reduces rancidity; discoloration and deterioration of certain food products (e.g. canned fruits and baked goods). Also many early stage products of the Maillard reaction (in which sugar is involved) have been shown to work synergistically with other natural antioxidants (e.g. vitamin E) to prevent oxidation of lipids and proteins, extending the shelf life of food.

• **Color** – Sugar can give color to the food product by Millard reaction andCaramelization. The Maillard reaction occurs between sugar and amino acids and gives rise to browning and flavoring in products such as bread, coffee, heated desserts and cakes. The end products of Maillard reaction include pigmentation, which causes coloration and aroma. Caramelization occurs when carbohydrates are exposed to high temperatures. The difference from Maillard reactions is no amino groups are involved. This reaction often occurs during the preparation of traditional sucrose syrups and caramels, which are extensively used in soft drinks, beer, confectionery and pastry products.

• **Texture** – The ability to interact with water and exist in amorphous and crystalline states gave the sugar functional properties to achieve desired texture in many food products. The molecules can reform either in a crystalline (from several micrometers to several millimeters) or an amorphous state (glassy, rubbery, gooey texture) depending on the processing of melted sugar. When the sugar added in enough amount to a solution, and bind water molecules, it will provide mouthfeel by increasing viscosity, and will decrease water activity, increase boiling temperature and decrease freezing temperature, so the behavior of proteins, starches, and hydrocolloids will change. Cotton candy is an example glass state of sucrose, taffies and caramels candies are example for "rubbery" plasticized form. In these candies, sucrose canbe replaced or partially substituted with other sugars or polyols.

• **Fermentation** – The sugar fermentation occurs by yeasts in anaerobic conditions, and produce carbon dioxide. This process is very important for bread making, beer and wine. In bread making, sugar plays important roles (in addition to taste), by leavening agent through the formation of carbon dioxide which causes bread dough to rise before and during baking, also the sugar has high affinity to bind to gluten so when dough is kneaded, a gluten structure of high elasticity forms, enabling the dough to stretch under the expansion of gases without collapsing.

CHAPTER III

SHORTENINGS

The term "shortening" technically refers to any type of fat that is solid at room temperature. This includes butter, margarine and lard. Shortening can be made from either animal fat or vegetable oil, but shortening made from partially or fully hydrogenated vegetable oil like soybean, cottonseed or refined palm oil, which are naturally flavoured liquid at room temperature and are more common nowadays. This makes it useful for applications where strong fat flavors are not desired. The chemical structure of the oil is changed through a process called hydrogenation (An extra hydrogen atom is added to vegetable oils which creates a solid fat). This causes the oils to become more solid, creating a thick texture that makes shortening good to use for specific types of cooking and baking.Although butter is solid at room temperature and is frequently used in making pastry, the term "shortening" seldom refers to butter, but is more closely related to margarine.

Shortening seems to get its name from the fact that it shortens gluten strands in wheat by adding fat. In other words it is used to prevent the formation of a gluten matrix by interfering with gluten formation in a dough's and batters to impart crisp, flaky and crumbly texture to baked products such as pie crusts and to increase the plasticity, or workability of dough's. However, some vegetable shortenings have artificial butter flavor added and are used as an inexpensive replacement for butter. Gluten creates a gummy or chewy end product, which is desired in elastic "long" doughs, such as that used for pizza crust. For flaky or crumbly "short" dough, the fat is worked into dry flour and creates a barrier between gluten molecules, thus preventing them from cross –linking once a liquid is added. Unlike butter, which separates into oil and milk solids when melted, shortening remains intact and reverts back to its soft, semi –solid state upon cooling. For this reason, cookies and other baked goods made with shortening tend to be soft, while those made with butter have a crispier texture.

Characteristics of shortening:

- They are 100 percent fat with a relatively high melting and smoking point.
- They are flavorless and odorless and create softness in the baking product.
- Oils they contain no animal products and so they are cholesterol –free and high in calories.
- They blend thoroughly throughout a mixture to form emulsion. It therefore coats more of the proteins, and the gluten strands produced are much shorter, a desirable result in short, crumbly, flaky and fine –textured products such as cookies, patties, muffins or chiffon cakes.
- They have higher degree of plasticity and therefore they can be easily shaped or molded.
- Helps in gaining the desired volume of the product.
- They are cheaper than other fats.
- They show higher resistance to oxidation and rancidity and therefore have a longer shelf life and can be stored at room temperature.
- Most of the shortenings are colorless, so a baker has ample opportunity to add any color according to his need.

• They easily distribute themselves in the entire product, so uniformity is attained.
• They can be melted or softened and creamed into a dough or batter.
• Shortening is used for creaming due to its ability to incorporate large volumes of air bubbles. This creates a fine, delicate structure in the end product.
• In cake making, it is used to tenderize the product by incorporating air in the finished cake batter as well as lubricating the other ingredients allowing the cake to rise more freely.
• Shortening imparts 'richness' to the eating quality of the cake.

CLASSIFICATION OF SHORTENINGS:

Shortenings may be conveniently and briefly classified in three groups– Animal, vegetable, and compound shortenings.

A. ANIMAL SHORTENINGS

Lard – is produced from selected fat of the hog through a process known as 'rendering'. It is a solid white product of almost 100 percent pure fat; it contains only a small amount of water. Lard yields flaky, flavorful pastries, such as pie crusts, but it is highly prone to rancidity. Since the development of modern shortenings, however, it is not often used in the bakeshop.

Butter – is the fat of milk, separated from milk or cream by churning and contains also a small amount of other milk constituents. Fresh butter consists of about 80% fat, about 15% water, and about 5% milk solids.

There are different types of butter available :

• **Unsalted butter** – It is more perishable, but it has a fresher, sweeter taste and is thus preferred in baking.
• **Salted butter** – It is butter with up to 2.5 percent salt added, which not only changes the butter's flavor, it also extends its keeping qualities. When salted butter is used, the salt content must be considered in the total recipe.
• **European –style butter or cultured butter** – contains more milk fat than regular butter, usually from 82 to 86 percent with very little or no salt. It is often churned from cultured cream, giving it a more intense, buttery flavor.
• **Whipped butter** – It is made by incorporating air into the butter. This increases its volume and spreadability but also increases the speed with which the butter will become rancid. Because of the change in density, whipped butter should not be substituted in recipes calling for regular butter.
• **Clarified butter** – It is butter in which water and milk solids have been removed by a process called clarification. It is although rarely used in bakery only when sometimes a more stable and consistent product is required to be achieved by using clarified butter.

<u>Butter has two major advantages in Bakery–</u>

1. Flavor – Shortenings are intentionally flavorless, but butter has a highly desirable flavor.
2. Melting qualities – Butter melts in the mouth. Shortenings do not. After eating pastries or icings made with shortening, one can be left with an unpleasant film of shortening coating the mouth.

<u>B. VEGETABLE SHORTENINGS</u>

It is made by hydrogenating (adding hydrogen to) vegetable oil, such as soybean or cottonseed oil. Vegetable shortenings are solid or semi –solid at room temperature and through the process of hydrogenation any desired degree of hardiness may be secured. They resemble the texture of butter but with virtually no flavor or odor. A high degree of perfection has been reached in the manufacture of hydrogenated shortenings which are very popular for cake work, and which possess excellent qualities. Example –Vanaspati ghee.

Oils – Oils are liquid fats. They are not often used as shortenings in baking because they spread through a batter or dough too thoroughly and shorten too much. Some breads and a few cakes and quick breads use oil as a shortening. Beyond this, the usefulness of oil in the bakeshop is limited primarily to greasing pans, deep –frying doughnuts, and serving as a wash for some kinds of rolls.

C. COMPOUND SHORTENINGS

Compounds, as the name signifies, represent that group of shortenings made by compounding of blending a vegetable oil with a hard fat in proper proportions so as to give a resulting product of desirable consistency similar to that of lard. Margarine, sometimes called 'artificial butter', is a mixture of animal or vegetable fats, usually refined oleo oil churned in with some butter, neutral lard, and milk. Sometimes, vegetable oils, such as cottonseed oil, are also used. Coconut oil is often used in the preparation of various kinds of so –called 'nut butter' or 'nut margarine'.

Flavorings, colorings, emulsifiers, preservatives and vitamins are added, and the mixture is firmed or solidified by exposure to hydrogen gas at very high temperatures, a process known as hydrogenation. Generally, the firmer the margarine, the greater the degree of hydrogenation and the longer its shelf life. Like butter, margarine is approximately 80 to 85% fat, 10 to 15% moisture, and about 5% salt, milk solids, and other components. But even the finest margarine cannot match the flavor of butter. Margarine melts at a slightly higher temperature than butter, making it useful for some rolled –in doughs such as puff pastry or Danish. Because they require higher temperatures to melt, margarine and other vegetable –based shortenings can leave a greasy taste on the tongue.

Storage of Shortenings:–

- Shortenings are always kept at a moist –free dark room at room temperatures. In very hot, humid storage environments, shortening may be refrigerated if desired, but it should be returned back to room temperature before using to ensure best results.
- Unopened airtight packed shortenings may last for 2 years.
- To maximize the shelf life of opened shortening, keep can tightly closed. An opened can of shortening will generally stay at best quality for about 1 year at room temperature.
- The best way is to smell and look at the shortening– if shortening develops an off odor, flavor or appearance it should be discarded.

CHAPTER IV

EGGS

The egg is a biological structure intended by nature for reproduction. It protects and provides a complete diet for the developing embryo, and serves as the principal source of food for the first few days of the chick's life. The egg is also one of the most nutritious and versatile of human foods.

The term egg not only applies to those of the hen, but also to the edible eggs of other birds such as turkey, geese, ducks, plover and gulls. But in hotel industry we are more concerned with hen's egg.

Composition:

A whole egg consists primarily of 04 parts i.e the outer shell, cell membrane, the white and the yolk.

The shell – The shell, composed of calcium carbonateis not only fragile but also porous, is the outermost covering of the egg. It prevents microbes from entering and moisture from escaping, and also protects the egg during handling and transport. The breed of the hen determines shell color; for chickens, it can range from bright white to brown. Shell color has no effect on quality, flavor or nutrition.

Cell membrane – It is found in the inner lining of the shell. It forms an air cell at the large end, and two white strands called chalazae on the either side hold the yolk at the center of the white.

Chalazae – These thick, twisted strands of egg white anchor the yolk in place. They are neither imperfections nor embryos. The more prominent the chalazae, the fresher the egg. Chalazae do not interfere with cooking or with whipping egg whites.

Egg white – It consists 2/3rd portion of the egg and is called Albumen. It is clear translucent liquid and contains sulfur and more than half of the albumin protein and riboflavin. The protein, which is clear and soluble when raw but coagulates and becomes firm and opaque at temperatures between 144°F and 149°F (62°C and 65°C) when coagulated.

The Yolk – It is the yellow portion of the egg. It constitutes just over one –third of the egg and contains three –fourths of the calories, most of the minerals and vitamins and all the fat. The yolk also contains lecithin, the compound responsible for emulsification in products such as hollandaise sauce and mayonnaise. Egg yolk solidifies (coagulates) at temperatures between 149°F and 158°F (65°C and 70°C). Although the color of a yolk may vary depending on the hen's feed, color does not affect quality or nutritional content.

In India eggs are graded according to the weight. There are 5 grades.

- Jumbo: more than 70 g,
- Extra large-60–70 g,
- large- 53-59 g,
- medium- 45-52 g,
- small- 38-42 g

The size of an egg does not affect the quality but does affect the price. Hence Bakers all over the world prefer the

Jumbo Sized eggs. Good eggs are available throughout the year but the best during the winter season.

Function of eggs in Bakery:

Eggs perform the following functions in baking –

• **Structure** – Like gluten protein, egg protein coagulates to give structure to baked products. This is especially important in high –ratio cakes, in which the high content of sugar and fat weakens the gluten. The dish must maintain that structure throughout the baking process. Some foods, like soufflés, will deflate soon after cooking as the air in them escapes, but other dishes, such as cakes, remain light and tall long after you remove them from the oven. Egg whites can be whipped to create egg white foam. This foam is filled with tons of air which helps to lighten and leaven baked goods.

• **Emulsifying** – Egg yolks contain natural emulsifiers like lecithin in the yolk and albumin in the whites that help produce smooth batters. Lecithin covers oil particles to keep them from gathering together once in the water – based mixture. By preventing the oil from clumping back together, the emulsifier prevents the finished product from separating. This action contributes to volume and to texture. Typical examples of emulsified mixtures are mayonnaise, salad dressing, baked goods, and ice creams.

• Leavening – Beaten eggs incorporate air in tiny cells, or bubbles. In a
batter, this trapped air expands when heated and aids in leavening. For
instance, the airy texture of an angel food cake would be impossible without

the leavening of the beaten whites. For maximum leavening power, use
room temperature egg whites, pristine bowls and beaters without any
grease, and a small amount of acid to stabilize the whites.

• **Tenderizing** – Gluten is a protein in the flour of baked goods. The long strands of gluten contribute to chewiness in finished products. Flours with higher gluten percentages have chewier textures, such as bread flour, whereas those with low protein content, such as cake flour, produce more tender products.

• **Shortening action** – The fat in egg yolks acts as a shortening. This is an important function in products that are low in other fats. When added to baked goods, the fat from yolks shortens the recipe's gluten strands, yielding a more delicate, toothsome result.

• **Moisture** – Eggs are mostly water. Moisture in baked goods prevents the products from going stale while improving the flavor and texture. Fats act as moisturizers in food, which the yolks contain. The proteins found in both the yolks and whites also contribute to holding moisture from the yolks in the finished goods. This moisture must be calculated as part of the total liquid in a formula. If yolks are substituted for whole eggs, for example, or if dried eggs are used, adjust the liquid in the formula to allow for the different moisture content of these products.Yolks also helpin binding ingredients together.

• **Thickening** – Eggs are valuable thickeners in the cooking of chiffon pie fillings and custard.

• **Wash** – Many types of bread use a wash to create a protein –rich coating that repels excess moisture while giving the loaf a shiny finish. Some foods that have toppings will use a wash of egg whites and water to hold the seeds, nuts, or grains in place during baking.

• **Flavor** – Without the richness of yolks, the tastes naturally in baked foods would not stand out as much. Eggs contribute flavor to baked foods.

• **Color** – Yolks impart a yellow color to doughs and batters.The carotenoid xanthophylls gives the yolks their distinctively bright color. Additionally, eggs also facilitate the Maillard reaction that occurs when proteins cook and brown. This browning occurs both in foods as well as on the surfaces of baked goods forming brown crusts.

• **Nutritional value** – they also enhance the healthfulness of foods with extra protein and fats and traces of essential minerals. Eggs do not include harmful trans-fatty acids but healthier monounsaturated and polyunsaturated fats.

• **Customer appeal**– Eggs enhance the appearance of products through their colour and flavour, and they improve texture and grain.

• **Shelf life** – The shelf life of eggs is extended through the fat content of the yolk.

Coagulation of eggs depends on:

• Intensity of heat more heat leads to faster coagulation.

• Heating time – more heating time leads to more coagulation.

• Presence of sugar and salt in the liquid salt aids in coagulation by lowering the coagulation temperature, whereas sugar increases coagulation temperature and helps in forming a firmer gel.

Foams:

Whipped egg whites are used to give lightness and rising power to soufflés, puffy omelets, cakes, some pancakes and waffles, and other products. The following guidelines will help you handle beaten egg whites properly.

• **Fat inhibits foaming** – When separating eggs, be careful not to get any yolk in the whites. Yolks contain fats. Use very clean equipment when beating whites.

• **Mild acids help foaming** – A small amount of lemon juice or cream of tartar gives more volume and stability to beaten egg whites. Use about 2 tsps cream of tartar per pound of egg whites (20 ml per kg).

• **Egg whites foam better at room temperature** – Remove them from the cooler 1 hour before beating.

• **Do not overbeat** – Beaten egg whites should look moist and shiny. Overbeaten eggs look dry and curdled and have lost much of their ability to raise soufflés and cakes.

• **Sugar makes foams more stable** – When making sweet puffed omelets and dessert soufflés, add some of the sugar to the partially beaten whites and continue to beat to proper stiffness. (This will take longer than when no sugar is added.) The soufflé will be more stable before and after baking.

MARKET FORMS:

1. **Fresh eggs or shell eggs** – These are most often used for breakfast cookery and are the main subject of this section.

2. **Frozen eggs** – These are usually made from high –quality fresh eggs and are excellent for use in scrambled eggs, omelets, French toast, and in baking. They are pasteurized and are usually purchased in 30 –pound (13.6 –kg) cans. These take at least two days to thaw at refrigerator temperatures.

• Whole eggs
• Whites
• Yolks
• Whole eggs with extra yolks

3. Dried eggs – Dried eggs are used primarily for baking. They are not suggested for use in breakfast cookery. Unlike most dehydrated products, dried eggs are not shelf –stable and must be kept refrigerated or frozen, tightly sealed.

• Whole eggs
• Yolks
• Whites

Purchasing quality of good eggs –

1. Colour – could be either brown or white but does not affect the quality of eggs.
2. Size and weight – Average weight of an egg is about 52 –55 gm and the weight of each egg is proportional to its size.
3. Egg Yolk Upstanding, well –rounded and of a good even color indicates freshness. The red spot on the yolk indicates that the egg is fertilized and it is prominent only when it is hatching.
4. Shell – Any cracks on the shell indicates deterioration of quality of eggs. The shell should be clean, well –shaped, strong and slightly rough.
5. Purchase only the amount needed for 1 2 weeks.
6. Buy farm fresh or refrigerated eggs.
7. Inspect carefully and discard any chipped ones.

Test for freshness –

1. Buouncy method – dip an egg in a glass of water, If it floats on top, it is fresh and if it sinks in the bottom, it is stale. In any stale egg, thick white gradually changes into thin white and the water passes from the white into the yolk. The yolk looses strength and begins to flatten resulting in evaporation of water and replacement of airinside. This causes the egg to float on the water.

2. Candling – When fresh eggs are held to the strong light, they have a uniform rosy tint and the yolk is firmly suspended in the center. The look more transparent on top. Stale eggs look cloudy and opaque and the yolk settles against the shell. Eggs having dark spots on the shell are definitely bad.

Preservation and storage of eggs:

The storage of shell eggs during the main laying season, in order to conserve them for consumption when they are scarce, has been practiced for many centuries. For the successful storage of eggs, the following conditions must be met.

• The eggs placed in storage must be clean; they must not be washed or wet.

• Packaging material used should be new, clean and odourless.

• Loss of water due to evaporation should be reduced to a minimum.

• The storage room must be free from tainting products and materials and should be cleaned regularly with odourless detergent sanitizers.

• The storage room must be kept at a constant temperature and humidity must be checked.

• There should be air circulation in the storage room.

• Eggs should be stored so that they are allowed to breathe.

• As far as possible, interior quality should be monitored; there should be a good proportion of thick white, the yolk should stand up well, and the flavour of white and yolk should be good.

• Recommended storage times –

1. Raw whole eggs – use by 'Best Before' date
2. Raw yolks or whites – use within 2 –4 days
3. Prepared egg dishes – use within 3 –4 days
4. Hard –cooked whole eggs – use within 1 week
5. Pickled eggs – use within 1 month
6. Frozen whole eggs (blended) – use within 4 months

"• ***In cold storage*** *–eggs are kept a little above freezing point under controlled humidity and flow of air. They can be kept upto 9 months.*

• ***Frozen eggs*** *– eggs broken in sterilized containers, pasteurized, packed and rapid frozen.*

• ***Dried eggs*** *– eggs broken, mixed well and then spray dried at 710C.*

• ***Greased eggs*** *– thoroughly cleaned and sanitized eggs are lapped with pure liquid grease dried and can be kept for 3 months. The grease seals the pores in the shell and prevents the eggs from deteriorating.*"

CHAPTER V

WHEAT AND FLOURS

Wheat is a cereal grain belongs to the genus triticum with 30,000 families. The kernel is 1/8 –¼ inches long, ovoid in shape, rounded in both ends. Along one side of the grain there is a crease, a folding of the aleurone and all covering layers. Wheat is consumed mostly in form of flour and small quantity s used in breakfast foods such as wheat flakes and puffed wheat. Other cereal grains include corn (maize), oats, rice, and rye.

Widespread consumption of cereal grains began in the Middle East about10, 000 years ago, when agriculture first began. It was then that wheat was first planted and cultivated. Today, thousands of varieties of wheat are grown throughout the world, most requiring fertile soil and a temperate climate. Several locations in North America have ideal conditions for growing high –quality wheat, including the Midwestern United States and the southern prairie region of Canada. Other major wheat growing countries include China, India, France, and Russia. Wheat is more popular than any other cereal grain for use in baked goods. Its popularity stems from the gluten that forms when flour is mixed with water.

Without gluten, raised bread is hard to imagine. Wheat is also preferred because of its mild, nutty flavor. Both factors, no doubt, account for wheat being the most widely grown cereal grain in the world.

Composition –

1. Carbohydrate 95 %
2. Proteins 5 %

3. Minerals 3%
4. Vitamins 1 %
5. Water 1 %

Classification of wheat:

Flour plays a major role in our bakery industry. The flour is obtained from wheat. So it is necessary to learn about wheat. Wheat is the most important cereal among all grains. We can get quality flour from good quality wheat. The quality of wheat depends upon the following.

1. Soil
2. Quality of seeds
3. Climate
4. Manure
5. Farming techniques

Wheat is classified into its (i) type, (ii) colour, and (iii) hardness

According to type, there are – –

- Triticumtriticum (also called hard wheat)
- Triticumcompectum (also called soft, wheat)
- Triticum durum (also called durum wheat)

The Tritium sativum wheat flour contains more proteins. This flour is used for the production of bread. The Tritium compectum wheat flour contains low protein. So it is used for the production of biscuits, cakes and pastries. The Tritium durum wheat is mainly used to prepare semolina and macroon.

According to colour –which is due to environmental factors –

1. Red wheat
2. White wheat
3. Yellow

According to hardness, wheat is classified into –

- Hard wheat
- Soft wheat

Hard Wheat: Bakery products are made from the hard type of wheat flour because it has the following characteristics –

1. High in protein
2. More water absorption power (WAP)
3. Good mixing capacity, that is, it is easy to mix
4. Fermentation tolerance
5. Good gas retention power
6. Falls into separate particles if shaken by hand
7. Feels slightly coarse and granular

Hence it is mainly used for yeast products (e.g. bread). Examples of hard wheat– (i) hard red winter, (ii) hard red spring and (iii) durum

Soft Wheat: Soft wheat flour contains the following characteristics –

1. Less protein
2. Less WAP
3. Poor mixing capacity
4. Poor fermentation tolerance
5. Tends to clump and hold together if pressed
6. Feels soft and smooth

Hence, it is mainly used to make biscuits, cakes and pastries. Examples of soft wheat– (i) soft red winter and (ii) soft red spring.

STRUCTURE OF WHEAT:

Wheat kernel: Wheat kernels are the seeds of the wheat plant, and they are the part of the plant that is milled into flour. Since cereal grains are in the grass family, wheat kernels can be thought of as a type of grass seed. In fact, when a field of wheat starts to grow, it looks like lawn grass. Wheat kernels have three main parts –

The endosperm– While whole wheat flour contains all three parts of the kernel, white flour is milled from the endosperm. Whole wheat flour is considered a whole grainproduct because it contains the entire wheat kernel. The endosperm makes up the bulk of the kernel. It is the whitest part, partly because it contains mostly starch–typically 70–75 percent starch. The starch is embedded in chunks of protein. Two important proteins in the endosperm of wheat kernels are the gluten –forming proteins, gluteninand gliadin. When flour is mixed with water, glutenin and gliadin form strands of gluten, important in the structure of baked goods. In fact, wheat is the only common cereal grain that contains sufficient glutenin and gliadin for the formation of good –quality gluten for bread making.

The germ– is the embryo of the wheat plant. Given the right conditions, the germ sprouts—germinates—and grows into a new plant Wheat germ is high in protein, fat, B vitamins, vitamin E, and minerals. These nutrients are important to the germ as it sprouts. While germ protein does not form gluten, from a nutritional standpoint it is of a high quality.

The bran– is the protective outer covering of the wheat kernel. It is usually darker in color than the endosperm, although white wheat, which has a light bran.

Types of flour:

Bakers use two primary types of white wheat flours– hard flour or strong flour and weak flour or soft flour. We get hard flour from hard wheat. It contains 11.2 – 11.8% protein, 0.45 –0.50% ash, 1.2% fat and 74 –75% starch. The higher protein found in strong flour indicates a higher level of gluten. This type of flour is mainly used for high –structured products like yeast products like yeast products, choux pastry and puff pastries. We get soft flour from soft wheat. This type of flour contains 8.4 –8.8% protein, 0.44 – 0.48% of ash, 1% fat and 76 –77% starch. Due to the less protein content, this flour is mainly used for low –structured products like biscuits, cakes, sponges, short and sweet paste. Apart from the above flours, there are other types of flour and they are classified according to their extraction rate.

Characteristics of good quality flour:

Bakers need good quality flour for production. Good quality flour should have the following characteristics:

Colour: The flour should be creamish white in colour. Good quality flour will reflect the light when it is shown to the light. Bleaching the flour helps to get the colour.

Strength: There are two types of flour– (i) strong and (ii) weak. The strength depends upon the gluten quantity present in the flour. Strong flour is preferred for making bread and weak flour is preferred for making cakes and confectionery products.

Tolerance: Tolerance is the ability of the flour to withstand the fermentation and/or the mixing process in excess of what is normally required to mature its gluten properly.

High absorption power: High absorption power means the ability of the flour to hold maximum amount of water. If the flour has less WAP the bread will not be of good quality and will have fewer yields.

Uniformity: If the flour is used un –uniformly, the quality of the product will differ. So constant monitoring and adjustment are required to get a satisfactory result.

Type of flours obtained from wheat:

The whole wheat grain consists of various components as discussed. Each of the components is milled in various proportions to yield different type of flours from the same plant and each one has a particular usage in the bakery kitchen. Let us discuss some of these flours.

Whole meal flour:

Also called atta in India, it is the whole milled wheat kernel. The flour is cream to brown in colour as it has the bran grounded with it. It is not advisable to sift the whole wheat flour as most of the bran, an important dietary component, will be lost.

Graham flour:

It is usually found in the USA and the milling concept of this flour is very interesting. The wheat kernel is separated into its various components such as endosperm, germ, and bran. The endosperm is ground finely to produce white flour with gluten, whereas germ and bran are ground till coarse. The milled flour is then mixed back to yield graham flour. In case of non –availability of this flour one can mix refined flour, bran, and germ in the ratios that they naturally exist in the grain.

Brown flour:

t is almost 85 percent of the grain millet, where some amount of bran has been extracted. It is nutritious as it has high percentage of germ.

Strong flour:

It is milled from hard flour, in other words from high protein flour. The strong flours absorb more water than weak flours, as gluten can absorb twice their own weight or water. This flour is used form products which will have a high rise in the oven such as yeast breads, choux pastry, and puff pastry. Strong flour is also known as baker's flour.

Weak flour:

Weak flour is also known as soft flour or cake flour. As the name suggests, this flour has less gluten and hence, it is used for products that need a softer texture such as cookies and cakes and sponges.

All purpose Flour:

The all purpose flour is a blend of flours and has medium strength. In India, all the refined flour that we get is all purpose flour. Cake flour Refer to weak flour.

Pastry flour:

It is a very finely ground polished flour of soft wheat kernels, usually enriched and bleached.

Self–raising flour:

This flour is usually of medium strength and contains baking powder in a proportion. Since the flour contains moisture, this can react with the baking powder lessening the effect of baking powder and hence, it is not advisable to buy the commercial self raising. This flour is commonly used to make afternoon cookies called scones.

Other Type of Flours:

Flours are not only derived from wheat but also from other grains and seeds. It is very important for chefs to have knowledge of such flours as they can make different products with the range of the flours which will be healthier. Also since many people are suffering from gluten allergies, it is important for chefs to use products which are gluten free. Many types of grains are available in the market but few of the popular
flours derived from them are discussed as below:

Rye flour:

Rye flour does not have as much gluten as in popular flour and hence, it is sometimes mixed in proportions with flour for the production of breads. Breads which use only rye flour are more dense and chewy. This flour is majorly used in the Russian and Scandinavian breads. Rye flour dough is quite heavy and sticky.

Spelt flour:

It is quite popular in European countries such as Germany, France, and Switzerland. It is made from spelt which is a species of wheat. It is good source of vitamin B.

Rice flour:

It is the finely ground polished rice with a similar texture of corn starch, usually used as thickening agent. Rice flour is free of gluten and if the dough has to be made one would have to make it with hot water.

Maize flour:

Popular in Mexico, this flour is made from cooked maize corn and then grounded. It is also known as Masaharina. This flour has also been used in India since time immemorial and a very popular north Indian dish called makki ki roti is made from it. This flour is also free from gluten.

Corn flour:

It is made by grounding the white heart or the germ of the corn kernel, one of the widely used thickening agents in Chinese cooking. This is also free of gluten and usage of this flour in products gives crispness to the product. It can also be added to strong flour to turn into weak flour. Commercial custard powder is also made with corn flour with colour and flavor added. Corn flour is not flour, but it is actually a starch.

Arrowroot:

This flour is finely milled from the arrowroot plant. It has the same properties as corn flour and the uses are very similar. It is widely used for making glazes.

Barley flour:

Made from the pearl barley, it has low gluten content with mild flavor.

Buckwheat flour:

It has distinctive grayish brown colour with earthy bitter taste. It is used to make classical preparations such as Russian blinis, pancakes, and French Galettes. In India it is widely eaten during fasts and is commonly known as 'kuttu ka atta'.

Gluten –free flour:

Apart from the flours discussed above, it is also very important for chefs to know about gluten –free flours, as the demand for the same are increasing constantly. Some of the gluten –free are discussed further.

Amaranth:

It is a green leafy vegetable related to spinach and beets. Tiny seeds of this plant are often ground into nutritious flour. It is light brown in colour and has a nutty aroma.

Rice flour Refer to description above.

Pulse flour:

These are the seeds of many edible legumes and can be ground into flours for use in gluten free breads. Chickpea flour is very commonly used in India and Mediterranean countries.

Maize flour Refer to description above.

Buckwheat Refer to description above.

Chestnut flour:

It is a smooth shelled nut it is usually roasted and ground into flour. In India it is called Singharey ka atta and is commonly eaten during fasting.

Barley flour:

Made from the pearl barley, it has low gluten content with mild flavor.

Cottonseed flour:

The seeds are commonly used for making margarines or cooking oils, but these seeds can be ground into flour which is quite nutritious.

Flaxseed flour:

It is an ancient seed which has been used in medicines from time immemorial. It is used whole toasted or ground into flour. It is believed to be a good cure for diabetic patients and is believed to lower cholesterol levels.

Millet Flour:

It can also grow in areas which do not get much rainwater. In India millets are commonly known as bajra.

Quinoa flour:

This is one of the grains which have the highest amount of protein. It is mainly fond in china; but its popularity is catching up with the western world as well.

Soybean flour:

It is high fat and high protein flour which has a strong distinctive nutty flavor.

Sunflowerseed flour:

It can be dried, roasted and ground into flour. It can be combined with other kinds of gluten free flour as it has a very nutty flavor.

COMPOSITION OF FLOUR:

Starch:

Starch is not soluble in water until it is heated to about 140 F with water of six times of its weight. Then the starch cells will swell and the cell wall will burst. Now the starch becomes soluble in water. This process is called gelatinization. Starch acts as filler as it gives rigidity to bread dough. It combines with lipids and gluten to retain the gas during fermentation. During milling 6% of starch cells are crushed and damaged due3 to the roller, type of wheat, moisture, etc. The water absorption power (WAP) of the flour mainly depends upon the damaged starch. Enzymes (alpha and beta amylases) act only on damaged starch to produce sugar for the yeast during fermentation. The damaged starch should not be more than 7 –9% for bread making. The damaged starch is not essential for cake or biscuit making. Hot bread directly from the over cannot be sliced immediately because the starch is not sufficiently stable and must be allowed to retrograde (slightly harden). When the bread cools down, starch cells shrink and become rigid so that the bread can be sliced easily.

Moisture:

An ideal moisture content of flour is 14% the source of moisture may be

tempering or the package materials or the humidity. If more moisture is in the flour it will

reduce the storage life, induce insect infestation, may get

fungus and bacteria and also will
reduce the WAP of the flour. This will result in fewer yields during production.

Protein:

Flour contains soluble and insoluble proteins, namely, 1. Albumin 2. Globulin 3. Gliadin 4. Glutenin

The soluble proteins (albumin and globulin) are useful in providing nourishment to yeast during the fermentation process for its growth and reproduction. The insoluble proteins, gliadin and glutenin form a rubbery material when water is added with flour. So when it is kneaded well, the rubbery material (texture) developed is called gluten. It gives structure to the baked products. While gliadin gives extensibility, glutenin gives strength and holds gas during baking. The quality of flour is decided by the gluten content. If the gluten content is more, then the flour will be suitable for high structured products like bread. This bread –making flour should have the gluten from 10% to 11.5%. If the flour contains less gluten, then the flour will be suitable for lower structured products like cakes and biscuits/cookies. This flour requires a low, that is, 7 –10% gluten content.

Ash:

The source of ash content in flour is bran. If the flour contains more ash, it means it has more bran. Too much ash gives dark colour to the flour and also cuts the gluten. Flour with higher ash content will not retain as much gas during different stages of processing and this affects the volume and gives poor texture to the products.

Sugar:

Naturally, flour contains a small quantity of sugar, namely, sucrose and maltose. It is used as yeast food to produce CO2 (carbon dioxide gas).

Fat or Lipids:

Fat or Lipids should not be more than 1% in flour. They contain the pigment carotene which gives colour to the flour. There is a higher quantity of oil/fat in the low grade flour than in the high grade ones. The fat or oil when separated from the flour is a pale yellowish liquid without taste or smell.

Enzymes:

Flour contains diastatic enzymes. They are alpha (A) amylase and beta (B) amylase. These enzymes hydrolyze starch and convert it into simple sugar. During fermentation, the simple sugar is used by the yeast to produce alcohol and carbon dioxide. The gas production depends upon the amount of enzymes found in the flour. Indian flours have less alpha amylase. These enzymes are necessary for producing good quality bread. In rain –damaged wheat, these enzymes will be available in excess. The bread made out of this flour will have dark crust colour and sticky c4rumbs. If these enzymes are less, the bread will have poor volume and dull crust colour.

WAP of flour:

The absorbing power of a flour is determined by weighing out 25 gms of flour into a suitable dish and adding water from a graduated burette, then properly making up the two dough separately to a certain standard consistency, which latter always must be alike for all samples tested. The number of cc and decimals of water used as indicated by the burette are multiplied by 4, and the product expresses the percentage of water – absorbing power.

This result is next confirmed by making a sample baking, using the proper amount of yeast, salt and other ingredients, taking care to make the dough of the same consistency as before. Weigh the dough carefully and make a notation of its weight. Next proceed to work the dough in the usual, but very careful, manner into bread. Immediately, upon drawing from oven, the bread is weighed, and the loss calculated. This gives the moisture –retaining power of flour. In order to get proper results, the sample dough must be carried at a uniform temperature, the length of fermentation must be always the same, and the same hold good for the heat of oven, which should be 425° F. Unless uniform conditions prevail, the retaining power of a flour will be affected.

MILLING OF WHEAT:

Preparation of raw wheat : As wheat arrives in the mill it is passed through a cleaning process to remove coarse impurities and is then stored according to its quality. This is mainly determined by the hardness, protein content and gluten quality of the wheat.

Cleaning:

Cleaning begins with screening to remove coarse and fine materials and the grain is separated by size, shape and weight. The finished product, whole pure wheat, is then passed into conditioning bins.

Conditioning:

Conditioning takes place before milling to produce uniform moisture content throughout the grain. Moistening helps to prevent break – up of the bran (hard outer layer) during milling and improves separation from the floury endosperm (the mass that forms the white flour of the grain).

Gristing:

After conditioning, different batches of wheat are blended together (gristed) to make a mix capable of producing the required flour quality.

Milling :

In India milling is done through stone grinding, but modern flourmills are with more mechanized to give pure wheat flour. The process involves the following –

1. Vibrator screen – (Thresher) – this removes bits of straw and other coarse materials and the second screen sieves foreign materials like unwanted seeds.

2. Aspirator – Here the wheat is cleaned by suction. The stream of air sucks lighter impurities like dust and stones.

3. Disc separator – catches individual grains of wheat but rejects larger or smaller materials.

4. Scourer – In this the beaters attached to the central shaft throws the wheat violently against the surrounding drum, resulting breaking of kernel hairs.

5. Magnetic separator – pulls out any metal particles present.

6. Washer stone – Here the wheat is washed, resulting precipitation of stones, clay and lighter materials float leaving only clean wheat.

7. Tempering – In this the wheat is exposed to moisture and then dried.

8. Entoleter – In this the degraded quality kernel is removed.

9. Grinding bin – Here the first break of wheat takes place

10. Shifter – Here the flour is shifted through cloth or fine sieve, giving wheat flour.

11. Purifier – in this the coarse grains are subjected to controlled flow of air, which lifts the bran leaving behind refined grains, which are separated, again by their size and

quality.

12. The down purifier – Here the final shifting is done and the grains are separates

The process is repeated over and over again. Shifters, purifiers reducing the rolls until the maximum amount of flour is separated consisting of at least 72 % of wheat.

Uses of wheat –

- Wheat flour – to prepare breads.
- Refined flour (maida) – loaf, breads and nuns, sweets.
- Semolina – Halwa. Pasta.
- Macaroni products – noodles, pastas.
- Cracked wheat – porridge.

The milling process –

Milling means the conversion of wheat into flour. There are two methods of milling –

1. Stone or home milling
2. Roller flour milling
3. Turbo milling

1. Stone milling:

Stone milling is an ordinary method of milling. Here two circular thick stones with rough surfaces are used, one lying on top of the other. This rough surface helps crush the wheat. Thus the wheat is converted into flour. This is known as whole meal flour. It contains bran, germ and endosperm. The following are the qualities of the whole meal flour –

- It has more nutritive value.
- The colour of flour is dark.
- It has less shelf life.

• Small stone particles may be present in the flour.
• The bread made from this flour gives delicious flavour.

2. Roller milling:

Roller milling is a commercial milling of wheat. Before milling the wheat, the following steps have to be followed –

Cleaning:

The object of cleaning the wheat is to

• Obtain pure flour and
• Avoid damaging the milling machineries

If the foreign particles like stone, barley, oats and iron are not removed, the quality of flour will be affected and iron rods may damage the machines causing heavy loss.

CLEANING STAGES:

Sieving– This process will remove the larger and smaller particles like damaged wheat, stone and husk

Magnetic separator– It removes the iron and steel particles.

Aspirator – The lighter impurities are removed using air currents.

Disc separator– This is used to separate barley, oats and other foreign material.

Scrubbing– Beard on the wheat is removed by brushes.

Tempering – After cleaning, the wheat is sprayed with water and left to be soaked for sometime, a process called tempering. The time of tempering varies according to the hardness of wheat.

The following are the merits of tempering

1. The moisture content of wheat is increased.
2. The burn become elastic and the endosperm become soft, so it makes barn removal easier.
3. The endosperm is made more friable which reduces soft, so it makes barn removal easier.
4. Germ also is rendered tough and flaky for easy removal.

The milling process has two stages –

1. Break milling
2. Reduction milling

Break milling: Break milling is the first operation in the milling process. After tempering, the wheat passes through two horizontal steel break rollers. The rollers rotate in opposite directions. The surface of the roller is rough, one rollers 3/2 time faster than the other. The break milling is done in the 4th and 5th stages. The first set of roller just cracks the wheat grain. Then they are passed through the series of break roller. And from the last series of the process, break flour and sooji and rava or semolina are obtained. The break flour in the first three stages is also known as patent flour.

Reduction milling: After the break milling process, the rest of the semolina is passed through the reduction rollers. The surface of this roller is smooth. They also rotate in opposite direction but the speed is lesser than the break rollers. In the first stage we get some semolina germ and barn. The next reduction roller crushes the semolina into fine and the bran and flattened germs are removed. The flour, thus obtained is called straight run flour.

3. Turbo milling:

Developed in 1950 is probably the greatest milling advances of the end century, because it gives us the opportunity to separate starch particles into different fractions and then blend the fractions into the desired ratio. This type of milling enable us to make custom blend flours for bread making, cake making, cookie making and other works.

Bleaching: The flour obtained after the milling process is called green flour. It contains high moisture and slightly yellowish colour due to xanthophylls. The fresh flour is not suitable for making bakery products. It has to be bleached by oxidation. Bleaching agents like chlorine, chlorine dioxide and benzyl peroxide are used to bleach the flour. The bleached flour is creamish white in colour.

Maturing: The fresh flour has poor water absorption power, poor strength and poor baking quality. It is improved by the oxidation process known as maturing. Chemicals like potassium bromated and ascorbic acid are used for maturing and to improve the above qualities.

By-products of wheat:

There are many by product of wheat used in the kitchen in one form or the other. They may be –

- **Whole wheat:** Unrefined or minimally processed whole –wheat kernels
- **Cracked wheat:** Coarsely crushed, minimally processed wheat kernels
- **Bulgur:** Hulled, cracked hard or soft wheat, parboiled and dried kernels
- **Semolina:** Grounded polished wheat kernels with bran and germ removed
- **Couscous:** Semolina pellets, often par cooked
- **Farina:** Polished medium ground wheat cereals
- **Bran:** Separated outer covering of wheat kernels and flaked or powdered
- **Germ:** Separated embryo of wheat kernels, flakes

Flour is one of the structural ingredients used in pastry and bakery kitchens. There are many different kinds of flours used in the pastry kitchen and each flour has a different role to play in the final outcome of the product.

Therefore it becomes important to choose the right type of flour for the right type of product. You would commonly hear chefs using words like strong flour and weak flour. These words merely indicate the amount of gluten present in the flour. There are two types of non –soluble proteins in the flour –"glutenin" and "gliadin". When the dough is kneaded these two proteins combine to produce gluten in the dough. Without gluten there will be no such thing as raised bread. Gluten provides elasticity to the dough, which in turn traps the air and gas released by yeast and forms a sponge –like texture in the baked breads. The gluten in the flour can be altered by various methods. Manipulating the dough for longer duration of time or adding some acid, such as lemon juice, will strengthen the gluten strands and time or adding some acid, such as lemon juice, will strengthen the gluten strands and addition of oils and fats will soften the gluten. Gluten can also be procured from the market as a commercial product and added to weak flours to increase their strength. It is almost impossible to knead corn flour and rice flour into dough as they have no gluten at all. Let us discuss some of the flours obtained from the wheat kernel in as they are commonly used in confectionery.

DIFFERENCES BETWEEN SEMOLINA, WHOLEWHEAT FLOUR AND REFINED FLOUR:

Semolina – This is the coarsely ground endosperm (no bran, no germ) of durum wheat. Its high protein content makes it ideal for making commercial pasta, and it can also be used to make bread. Semolina flour is made with grooved steel rollers. Semolina has very high gluten content and the flour has a substantial amount of protein.

Whole wheat flour – Since roller milling separates the bran and the germ from the endosperm; the three components actually have to be reconstituted to produce whole – wheat flour. Because of the presence of bran, which reduces gluten development, baked goods made from whole –wheat flour are naturally heavier and denser than those made with white flour. Many bakers combine whole –wheat and white flour in order to gain the attributes of both.

Refined flour – Maida is a type of wheat flour from India. Finely milled without any bran, refined and bleached, it closely resembles Cake flour. Owing to this wide variety of uses, it is sometimes labeled and marketed as "all –purpose flour", though it is different from all – purpose flour as commonly understood in the US, where it is made from the endosperm (the starchy white part) of the grain. The bran is separated from the germ and endosperm which is then refined by passing through a sieve of 80 meshes per inch (31 meshes per centimeter). Although naturally yellowish due to pigments present in wheat, maida is typically bleached, either naturally due to atmospheric oxygen, or with any of a number of flour bleaching agents.

Storage of flour:

If moisture is allowed to get into the flour, it may cause it to become clumpy. In some cases, flour can attract psocids (tiny brown or black insects which live in dry foods) and cankers. The flour will itself sweat (absorb moisture), resulting in the formation of inferior products. For proper storage of the flour, the following things should be kept in mind –

1. The storage area should be well ventilated.
2. Hessian cloth or jute cloth is always preferred so that it can allow air to go in.
3. Flour bags should be piled off the floor on wooden

boards to enable free circulation of air all around the piles.

4. Should be kept away from direct sunlight.
5. Should be stored away from foreign odours because it picks up these odours easily.
6. Avoid insect infestation.
7. Should be stored in dry clean bins with fitting lids.
8. Temperature of the storage area should be 19 –240 C
9. The relative humidity should be 55 –65%. Too low or too high relative humidity is detrimental to flour quality.
10. The containers should be clearly labeled with their content so as to avoid mistakes when selecting the correct flour for use.

FLOUR TESTING:

These are the several methods for testing the flour.

Test for water absorption power (WAP): Take 100 gms of flour and mix 50 ml of water. Mix it well. If the dough is stiff, add 1 ml of Take 100 gms of flour and mix 50 ml of water. Mix it well. If the dough is stiff, add 1 ml of water at a time and mix until it becomes a pliable dough. After obtaining this quality, note the quantity of water added. This quantity will be the WAP of the particular flour. More protein flour has more WAP. It will increase the number of portion (yield).

Test for the quality of gluten in flour: Take some quantity of flour and mix it with enough water. Knead it well to get smooth dough. Then put this dough in water for 30 minutes at room temperature. Then take it out and wash it in the running water till the starch is completely removed. Squeeze the dough until it gives no white streaks, and what remains is called gluten. Squeeze out to remove the excess water and this is known as wet gluten. It can be expressed as a per cent of the flour sample. Then keep the wet gluten in a cool oven (140 C) till all the moisture is evaporated. Now it is called dry gluten. The dry gluten weight should be 1/3 of the wet gluten. For example – If the wet gluten is 30 gms, the weight of dry gluten should be 10 gms. If the dough in the oven rises, the flour will be considered to have a good quality of gluten.

pH value: pH value indicates the acidity or alkalinity. It is measured from 0 to 14.7 is neutral. When the ph is above 7, it is called alkaline. When it is below 7, it is acid. The pH value should be 5.5 –6.5 for bread making and 4.5 –5 for high –ratio cakes. However, some cakes are in the alkaline side.

CHAPTER VI

MILK AND MILK PRODUCTS

Milk:

Milk may be defined as the whole fresh lacteal secretion obtainedby the complete milking of healthy animals excluding that from the animals that are within 15 days or after 15 days of calving. Milk most often means the nutrient fluid produced by the mammary glands of female mammals. The female ability to produce milk is one of the defining characteristics of mammals and provides the primary source of nutrition for newborns before they are able to digest more diverse foods. It is also processed into dairy products such as Cream (food) cream, butter, yogurt, icecream, gelato, cheese, casein, whey protein, lactose, condensed milk, powdered milk, and many other food –additive and industrial products. Other than cows and buffalo, milk can also be obtained from sheep, goats, horses, donkeys, camels, yaks, water buffalo and reindeer. Whale milk, though not used for human consumption has the highest fat content
in mammals.

The other forms of milk are –The white juice and the processed meat of the coconut in more –or –less liquid form, used especially in Thai, Indian, and Polynesian cuisine. A non –animal substitutes such as rice, soy milk etc. are also used.

Nutritive composition: The milk contains calcium necessary for the bone formation and teeth. It contains certain vitamin such as vitamin A and D, vitamin B –1, B –12 and vitamin C the last one is smaller amount. It is also rich in protein fat and carbohydrate and the rest 87% is water.

Human milk contains, on average, 1.1% protein, 4.2% fat, 7.0% lactose (a sugar), and
supplies 72 kcal of energy per gms .

Cow's milk contains, on average, 3.4% protein, 3.6% fat, and 4.6% lactose, and supplies 66
kcal of energy per 10 gms.

<u>Curdling of milk:</u> Milk curdles naturally or made to curdle. Milk contains lactose and when raw milk is kept standing for few hours, the bacteria (lactobacillus) starts fermentation resulting the formation of lactic acid which causes the casein which is held in solution by the calcium to separate and to be simply thrown down without making further changes in a mass known as curds and the liquid left behind is called whey. Curdled milk is used to make cheese and curd.

<u>There are four periods of milk decay –</u>

1. Rancid (also called on the turn. Milk is still consumable at this stage)
2. Curdling (separation of curd and whey will occur but may still be consumable)
3. Coagulation (beyond use. A period of aromatic decay sets in accompanied by mould.
4. Dry (beyond use. The milk has dehydrated and become hard and chalky)

<u>TYPES OF MILK PRODUCTION:</u>

1. **Pasteurized milk:** By this method the bacteria is killed and their action of sour producing is retarded.

Pasteurization is done by two ways –

> "*a) Flash process –In this milk is heated to 71.1oC (161o F) and then subsequently held for 15 seconds and then it is rapidly cooled below 48oC (50o F).*
> *b) Hold process –In this the milk is heated to 63 –65o C (145 –150o F) and then maintain this temperature for 3minutes and then cooled down immediately to 48o C (50oF)*"

2. **Homogenized milk:** In this milk and cream are mixed together briskly so that they do not separate when stand. This is done by subjecting the milk high pressure (200lb) per sq. inch through a small apparatus so that the fat globules are reduced in size and increase in number, which results in easy mixture and the fats do not rise above to the surface.

Advantages of homogenized milk –

1. Do not need mixing of fat and milk
2. Can be stored considerably for a longer period of time.
3. More palatable
4. Can be easily modified for infant feeding.
5. The viscosity of the milk increases.
6. Softer curd and cheese is formed.
7. Stiffer custards can be prepared.

Dis –advantage

- It curdles the soup.
- In a sauce the fat can be separated.

3. **Sterilized milk:** This is homogenized milk in which the milk is heated to 104 –1100C for 30 –40 minute in sealed bottle or cans, which kills the souring and disease

bearing bacteria. It has a different taste from fresh milk and the shelf life of this type of milk is 2 – 3 months in sealed conditions.

4. **Ultra – heat treatment milk** : In this the milk is treated to ultra –heat treatment that is 1320C for 1 second under sterile conditions. Shelf life is of 2 –3 months.

5. **Condensed milk** : It is richer than evaporated milk because more water has been removed. It may be sweetened or unsweetened, but sugar acts as preservation which is added in form of sucrose or dextrose.

6. **Dried milk**: Can be produced either by – **Roller Drying** – The evaporated milk is run on to hot rollers which cause the removal of remaining moisture by further evaporation the solid milk which sticks to the roller in scraped off the roller. The temperature and the rate of rotation of the steel heated drums are controlled so that the milk is dried in less than a complete rotation. **Spray Drying** – By this the milk is evaporated, to reduce the bulk, then it is forced through a fine spray into a hot chamber and here in the hot chamber the remaining water is removed. The temperature ranges from 3800F to 4000F. It is desirable to cool down the fired. Powder as quickly as possible in a separate cool room, because the prolonged temperature will deteriorate and discolour the product.

7. **Skimmed Milk**:It is that from which a part whole of their fat has been removed in the
form of cream. Skimming of milk is done by machine, called separator, which applies the
centrifugal force to remove the milk fat and often 1% of fat remains in the milk after
skimming.

Milk Products :

a) Cream

b) Yoghurt and fermented milk(cultured milk – sharp taste, 5% fat and Smetana – cultured milk containing 10% fat)
c) Cheese and Paneer
d) Butter
e) Khoya

Storage of milk :

- As milk gets curdled, it should not be kept standing for not more than approx. 1 hour.
- Keep milk in refrigerated conditions
- As milk absorbs odor from other items easily and gets contaminated, so extreme precautions are taken. Milk should be always be kept covered.
- Frozen milk should be thawed first and then boiled
- Always boil the milk, cool and then refrigerate. Boiling kills all the harmful micro –organisms.
- Pasteurized milk will keep upto 5 days under refrigeration.
- Unopened sterilized milk can be kept for up to several days.
- Dried milk is stored in air –tight containers and kept in cool dry place.
- The storing container should be fresh without any swills or odor.
- Self –live in refrigerator in frozen condition is approx 4 –5 days.
- Tinned milk should be stored in cool, dry place.

Cream:

Cream is the lighter weight portion of milk which still contains all the main constituents of milk but in different proportions. The fat content of cream is higher than that of milk and the water content and other constituents are low.

Cream is separated from the milk and heat treated.

Two characteristics of cream are important to the cook; its taste, whether sweet or nutty (as with crème fraiche), and its fat content. Most cream is sweet; it has been pasteurized or ultra –pasteurized (sterilized), thus destroying disease causing bacteria and enzymes so the odour and flavour remains mild. In some countries, preservatives may be added that can further detract from the fresh flavour of sweet cream. Pasteurized or sterilized creams may also be homogenized to produce a smoother texture. Crème fraiche, on the other hand, has a strong flavour.

Crème Fraiche –When unpasteurized cream is left to stand, it develops a full slightly sour taste that mellows and intensifies over time. This is crème Fraiche, the standard crème in France.

Clotted Cream – as its name implies, clotted cream often called Devonshire or Cornish cream, has a different texture from other creams. To make it unpasteurized milk is left to stand until the cream rises to the surface, then heated so that the cream sets and can be skimmed off. The cream is pasteurized before sale. Creamy yellow, with a buttery texture and a fat content of over 55 %, clotted cream is famous in Britain, served with scones and strawberry jam and it makes an excellent accompaniment to fresh or poached fruit.

Reconstituted Cream – It is made by emulsifying butter with skimmed milk or skimmed milk powder. This is not true cream, but a substance which resembles it in appearance. The fat content of the cream determines its richness and whipping characteristics.

Non –dairy cream: There are several types and qualities available which are produced from an emulsion of oil, margarine or butter with milk powder, water and other permitted substances.. Non –dairy creams can be used for filling and decorating small and large cakes and making and finishing sweet dishes.

Yoghurt:

Yoghurt is a cultured milk product made from cows, ewes', goats' or buffaloes' milk. Differences in the taste and texture of the product depend on the type of milk used and the activity of the micro –organisms involved. A bacterial 'starter culture' is added to the milk which causes the natural sugar 'lactose' to ferment and produce lactic acid.

There are two types of yoghurt –

- Stirred yoghurt, which is smooth fluid consistency
- Set yoghurt, which is more solid and has a firmer texture.

All yoghurts are 'live' and contain live bacteria which remain dormant when kept at low temperatures, unless it clearly states on the packaging that it has been 'pasteurized', sterilized or ultra –heat –treated'. If stored at room temperature or above, the dormant bacteria become active again and produce more acid. Too high acidity kills the bacteria, impairs the flavour and causes the yoghurt to separate.

Types of yoghurt :

- Fat free yoghurt – contains less than 0.5% milk fat
- Low fat yoghurt – contains 1.5% milk fat
- Whole milk yoghurt – contains 3.8% milk fat
- Whole or real fruit yoghurt – contains whole fruit in sugar syrup

- Fruit flavoured yoghurt – contains fruit juices and syrups.
- Natural yoghurt – contains no colour, preservatives,, stabilizers or thickeners and may be fortified with vitamins.

Storage of yoghurt :

• Yogurt, as a dairy product, can spoil quickly if it is not properly stored. Bacteria grow at room temperature and yogurt must remain refrigerated at temperatures in between 34 to 40 degrees.

• Once cut opened, it should be used within three to four days.

• Prevent cross –contamination – Rather than eating it straight out of the pot, scoop some into a bowl and eat it from there. Also, every time you use it, make sure you use a clean spoon, so a bacterium doesn't contaminate your yoghurt. As a precaution, you should also avoid mixing fresh and used yoghurt.

• Use an airtight container to protect your yoghurt from strong odours.

• Don't store it in the door of your fridge – Keep your yoghurt fresh by being efficient and keeping it at the back of the fridge, where temperatures stay cool and consistent. Due to its delicate nature, small changes in temperature can affect the longevity of it.

• Freeze it – Although freezing yoghurt changes its texture in a way that might not make it suitable for eating, it can still be used as an ingredient to bake up a delicious cake.

• Expiration Date – Yogurt is sold with an expiration date, or a "sell by" date. These dates should be taken into consideration. Never buy yogurt that is past its expiration date.

Cheese:

A solid food obtained from the pressed curdfrom the wholly, partially or skimmed milk of cow or from the any milk producing animal, like buffalo, ewe, goat, sheep, camel etc., it is often seasoned and aged. It is a generic term for a diverse group of fermented milk –based food products. Cheese is produced throughout the world in wide –ranging flavors, textures, and forms.

It is obtained by coagulating milk with rennet, lactic acid or other suitable enzyme or acid with or without further treatment of separated curd by heat or pressure or by means of ripening ferments, special moulds of seasonings. But the most commonly used technique is to use the action of rennet on milk. Curd formed at 106F is more firm whereas at low temperature the curd is soft.

Rennet is obtained from the gastric juices of calves and in the inner lining of the stomach. Rennet precipitates the casein of the milk to form curd. The coagulation of casein may also be brought by the addition of certain acids. The rennet formed curd is firm and elastic where as acid formed curd is sticky.

Origin : The origins of cheese have not been documented. One does not know where or when it came into existence, but the farmers of Mesopotamia, who first domesticated goats and sheep certainly made their cheese from milk. There is a story –around 900years ago; an Arabian merchant was riding on a camel through the desert. He had brought with him a bag of skin that was filled with goat milk. When he opened the bag to drink the milk, he found that the milk had converted to cheese. Apparently, the heat and rocking motion of the camel had turned the milk into solid cheese and whey. Cheese is made by almost every country in the world. There are varieties of cheese with different textures, flavours and colours. Though cheese is primarily made of cow's milk but in certain parts of Europe and the Middle East, it is also made of goat's milk. Other sources for making cheese are the milk of yak (China), buffalo (Philippines, India and Italy) and even from donkey and horse's milk in Afghanistan and Iran.

Nutritive Value of Cheese: Cheese, like many other milk products, provides protein, vitamins, minerals, fat, saturated fat and cholesterol. While cheese is one of the best sources of calcium, it may also be high in sodium and saturated fat.1 gms. Serving of natural cheese supplies the same amount of calcium as 110ml. of milk or yogurt, as well as 12 to 14 gm. total fat, gm. saturated fatty acids, 44 ml. cholesterol and 173 calories. For sodium, while 10ml of milk contains 12ml, 1 gm of natural cheese could contain from 11 to 45ml, while 2 gm of process cheese could contain 80ml.

Making of Cheese: Milk is heated to a certain degree depending upon the type of curd required. The rennet is then added to this milk, which takes 8 –1hours to coagulate all the milk casein and removing the whey. When all the whey is removed, the curd mats together and forms mould which is left for ripening. Ripening helps to improve the flavour, texture and the colour of the cheese. The ripening period may vary from weeks to years depending upon the quality desired. Then the cheese is stored which are called curing, which again depends upon the period of the storage. The longer the curing period, the sharper, richer and flavourful cheese is developed. In the process of ripening cheese looses its toughness, rubbery qualities and becomes soft and mellow. During ripening process the bacterial action takes place, which produces CO2 , which produces holes and veins in cheese.

Classification of cheese: A cheese can be distinguished by its flavor, smell and texture. Fresh cheese is un –ripened curd eaten shortly after it is made, while soft cheese is briefly ripened and can be easily spread and is also very fattening. Semi –Hard cheese is matured with less moisture and is pretty easy to cut and hard cheese is matured over a long period with less moisture content and may have up to 50% fat.

Fresh and Soft Cheese :

1. **Cottage Cheese or Paneer** – A lumpy and bland curd cheese, usually containing cream, has a moist texture. It is available in most countries and is used mainly for making cheesecakes and salads. In India, cottage cheese is very commonly used in most houses and goes by the name of 'paneer'.

2. **Cream Cheese** – This cheese is prepared in the same way that cottage cheese is made but only from full –cream cow's milk. There are different types of Cream Cheeses – they could be double cream cheese and singles cream cheese. White and smooth, cream cheese is usually used for snacking and spreading.

3. **Curd Cheese** – 'Curd' is the general name given to all un –ripened cheeses made from the separated curds of cow's or goat's milk. Curd cheese has a slight acidic taste and is used in the preparation of sweets and savory fillings. It is also used to make dips and spreads and is available in

most countries easily.

4. **Mozzarella** – This Italian un –ripened curd cheese was originally made from buffalo milk but now is made from cow's milk as well. This is an extremely soft cheese with a chewy texture and has a mild and creamy taste. This cheese is used primarily to make pizzas, lasagna and grilled sandwiches.

5. **Ricotta** – Another Italian un–ripened cheese made from the whey ofcows milk. This cheese is very smooth and has a milky taste and is used for the preparation of sweets and savory dishes as well as for making pizzas.

Semi Hard Cheese:

1. **Cheshire** – An English specialty made of cow's milk with a crumbly texture and a salty ting. This cheese ripens at a fast rate. Cheshire cheese is available in two varieties – Red Cheshire and White Cheshire. It makes a very good snack cheese.
2. **Emmental** – This world famous Swiss cheese is made of cow milk and has a slight sweet and nutty taste. It is usually used as a base for fondues and toasted snacks.
3. **Dunlop** – This is a Scottish cheese, made of cow's milk with a bland and buttery taste. It is an ideal snack cheese and is good for toasting.
4. **Gruyere** – This is a Swiss cheese but variations are produced in France and Switzerland. It has a smooth and uniform paste with a few pea –sized holes and a dark brown rind. It is a good table cheese and is used to make fondues, sauces and quiches.
5. **Cheddar** – This cheese by far is England's most famous. Made from cow's milk, it varies from mild to very sharp. Cheddar cheese is used mostly for cooking and also made

for making sauces, souffles, salads and pizzas.

Hard and Smoked Cheese :

1. **Parmesan** – An Italian cheese with a grainy texture and a golden color, it is made of finely cut and carefully separated curd, which then is stirred and scalded before being pressed. It has a sharp and salty flavor. Parmesan cheeses are used for Italian cooking.

2. **Sapsago** – A Swiss cheese made from sour and skimmed milk, is also known as green cheese because of its pale green color.

3. **Smoked Emmental** – This cheese is traditionally made in a long sausage like shape and is used often as a snack cheese.

4. **Mycella** – A Danish cheese that's made from cow's milk and has blue –green streaks. It's a relatively mild blue cheese, and is usually used as a table cheese but can also be used in salads and salad dressings.

Blue Cheese :

1. **Danish Blue** – Danablu or Danish Blue is made from homogenized cow's milk. This cheese is creamy and soft textured and has a very strong taste. It makes a very good dessert cheese.

2. **Blue Cheshire** – A cylindrical and blue version of the Cheshire and the finest of all blue cheeses, this is made from cow milk and ripens and turns blue 'accidentally'. With a very rich taste, it is best used as a dessert cheese.

3. **Bavarian Blue** – A double creamed, soft and blue –veined cheese with a mildly sour taste, it is best used in sandwiches as a spread.

4. **Blue Castello** – This is a rich, moist, and creamy blue cheese. It's fairly mild and a good choice for unadventurous guests.
5. **Gorgonzola** – Italian Gorgonzolas are creamy and mild, while domestic versions are sharper and more crumbly. A Gorgonzola dolce is young, creamy, and mild, while a Gorgonzola naturale = mountain Gorgonzola is aged until it's firmer and more pungent. Use within a few days after purchasing. For best flavor, serve at room temperature.

Storage of Cheese :

1. Once you've brought the cheese home, leave it in its original packaging and tightly cover it in plastic wrap. This reduces air circulation, which in turn reduces the possibility of mold. Store the cheese in the coldest part of your refrigerator – not on the door.

2. Cheese is more flavorful at room temperature. Let it stand for a half hour before serving.

3. Cheese will continue to ripen, no matter how carefully it is stored. Hard cheeses will generally keep for several months, whereas softer cheeses will keep from one to three weeks after opening, if stored in an airtight container.

4. Shredded cheese is more prone to mold because it has more exposed surface area. Try to use shredded cheese within a few days.

5. Use moisture –proof and airtight wrapping.

6. Freeze quickly and store at F for two to six months.

7. Thaw in refrigerator so cheese won't lose moisture; the slower the cheese is

thawed, the better.

8. Use as soon as possible after thawing.

Uses of Cheese in bakery :

• It is creaminess helps keep baked goods moist
• It is tanginess imparts a crave –worthy, old –fashioned flavor
• It is acidity helps activate baking soda , which can make baked goods fluffy and light
• It can step in for sour cream, mayonnaise or crème fraîche, bring in the same tangy with less guilt
• It can act as a garnish, in place of ice cream or whipped cream topping.

Purchase of cheese :

1. From well –known and reliable shopkeeper.
2. Inspect for any type of spoilage, breakage, mould formation, smell.
3. Inspect the package and labels.
4. You should have enough knowledge about the characteristics and texture of the cheese. Examine the cheese, especially the aroma, appearance, and flavor. An ammonia, sour milk, barnyardy or unclean aroma is undesirable. The cheeses should be characteristic of their style, with an interior that is free of cracks, discoloration, and mold (unless it is a blue cheese).
5. If possible taste the cheese before buying.

Butter :

Butter is the fat of cream that is separated – more or less – completely from the other milk constituents by agitation or churning. The mechanical rupture of the protein film around the fat globules allows the fat globules to clump together. Butter formation is an example of breaking of oil –in –water emulsion by agitation. The resulting emulsion that forms in butter itself is water –in –oil emulsion, with about 18% water being dispersed in 80% fat and a small amount of protein acting as an emulsifier. Most frequently made from cow's milk, butter can also be manufactured from the milk of other mammals, including sheep, goats, buffalo, and yaks. Butter is made from either sweet or sour cream.

Butter from sour cream has a more pronounced flavour. The cream may be allowed to sour naturally or may be acidified by the addition of pure culture of lactic acid bacteria to sweet cream, which produces a butter of better flavour and keeping quality. Salt and food colorings are sometimes added to butter. Rendering butter, removing the water and milk solids, produces clarified butter or ghee, which is almost entirely butterfat.

It consists of more than 80% butterfat and small amounts of protein, vitamin A and D, minerals, lactose and water. Butter must have a minimum of 80% fat content, a non –fat solid content of 8% and a maximum of 12% moisture (water).

Factors that affect quality of butter –

- The breed of animal (cow or buffalo) from which the milk was obtained.
- The type of feed that was available for the animal.
- The method of manufacture (fresh or ripened cream).

• The efficiency of manufacture (wrong temperature may affect the colour and flavour of butter).
• Whether or not the butter was blended.
• The addition of salt and colour.
• The method of packing and storing.

Classification of butter :

There are four main types of butter –

"• *Fresh or Sweet cream Butter,*
• *Ripened cream or Lactic butter,*
• *Blended or milled butter and*
• *Special Butter*"

(Fresh and ripened cream Butters are known as "Creamery butters").

Manufacture of creamery butter:

The manufacture of creamery butter takes place in four main stages, as mentioned –

1. **Holding** – The cream (35%) is pasteurized at 95°C (203°F) and held for 2 to 4 seconds. It is then cooled to 4.5°C (40°F) and held there for several hours to ensure the uniform hardening of the fat globules.

2. **Ripening** – When the end product is going to be a ripened butter or lactic butter, a "starter" (which is a laboratory culture of acid –producing bacteria) will be added during the Holding stage, in which the holding temperature will be 15.5 –18.5°C (60–65°F) for 3 to 4 hours before being cooled to 4.5°C (40°F). This gives the butter a much fuller flavour. However, the flavour tends to

fade and therefore the ripened cream butter has a shorter life than the sweet cream butters. This stage will be omitted when making the sweet cream butter.

3. **Churning** – The churning of cream is done in large stainless steel churns that hold about 1000 gallons of cream. The temperature must not exceed more than 4°C. The churns are rotated while internal rollers pass through the cream. This breaks the envelope of non –fat particles/ solids that surround the small fat globules and coalesce to form larger groups of butter fat. The envelope is dispersed in the thin liquid part of the cream to form buttermilk. After about 30 minutes of churning, the butter separates out in the form of grains and floats in the buttermilk. The buttermilk is carefully drained away and used for other purposes.

4. **Washing and salting** – The butter grains are now washed with ice water to remove any traces of buttermilk left on the surface of each grain, in order to maximize the keeping quality. Ice water also helps to harden butter grains. Salting can be done in two ways –

> "*a. By adding fine grains of dairy salt, and*
> *b. By soaking in a brine solution for 10 –15 minutes and allowing the butter to absorb it.*"

The quantity of salt added usually average 1% for ripened cream butter and 1.5% for fresh cream butter. Salt contributes to flavour and improves the keeping quality.

The butter grains are then worked into a smooth solid mass by rotating the churns slowly for 10 –15 minutes, then weighed and packed. Colouring (annatto) may also be added at this stage. If unsalted butter is required, the salting stage is omitted.

Blended Butter : Blended butter is a blend of butters from different regions or countries. These are mixed together to produce a product of standard quality at a competitive price, under a brand name.

Special Butters :

This group includes some butter that are not commonly available and those which are not true butters. These include –

1. Whey butter – Whey is the liquid which separates from the curd while making cheese. The butterfat obtained from the whey may be used to produce butter, or it may be added to fresh cream/milk prior to it being processed into butter. Due to its origin, this butter has a faint cheesy flavour.
2. Milk blended butter – Quantities of milk are blended into butter, thereby increasing the moisture content to 24% (max.).
3. Powdered butter – This is spray –dried butter containing 80% milk fat and non –fatty solids. It is produced on a large scale in Australia and is used mainly in the Bakery trade.
4. Compound butters – These are made by adding a particular natural flavour or colour to butter, depending on the type of food with which it is served. It is generally used as an accompaniment e.g. Lobster butter, Parsley butter etc.
5. Cocoa butter – This is not a true butter, rather obtained by crushing the cocoa beans. It is the most expensive ingredient used in chocolate making. Cocoa butter substitutes, using palm oil, are also available.
6. Peanut butter – It is a paste –like substance obtained by grinding roasted peanuts that may be further emulsified

and flavoured.

Uses of Butter :

1. As a spread for bread, toast and scones.
2. As a basic ingredient in pastry –making and cake –making.
3. Used as an accompaniment (compound butter).
4. To enhance the taste and flavour of soups and sauces.
5. As a cooking medium (The smoke point of butter fat is only 127 –130°C; so a vegetable oil should be used when high cooking temperatures are required).
6. For butter sculptures.

Purchase of butter:

1. Good quality butter should have a clean flavour and aroma characteristic the type of butter.
2. Have a close body, a waxy texture,
3. Be of uniform colour
4. Have a uniform distribution of salt (if added), be clean in appearance and have an absence of any free moisture.
5. Butter is available in 10 Gms, 100 Gms and 500 Gms packs in the market.

Storage of Butter:

1. Butter is a perishable product and tends to loose flavour and go rancid on prolonged storage. Exposure to sunlight can make it go rancid faster.
2. It must be stored at refrigerated temper from strong flavoured foods, for it absorbs odours and flavours easily.
3. If purchased in bulk, it can be frozen at

Khoya:

Khoa is a concentrated whole milk product obtained by open pan condensing of milk under atmospheric pressure. According to Food Safety and Standard Regulations 2011, Khoya, by whatever variety of names it is sold such as Pindi, Danedar, Dhap, Mawa or Kava, means the product obtained from cow or buffalo or goat or sheep milk or milk solids or a combination thereof by rapid drying. The milk fat content shall not be less than 30 percent on dry weight basis of finished product. It may contain citric acid not more than

0.1 percent by weight. It shall be free from added starch, added sugar a matter.

- Yield of khoa from cow milk = 17
- Yield of khoa from buffalo milk = 21

Manufacture of Khoa :

Khoa is made by simmering milk in an iron karahi for several hours, over a medium fire. The gradual vaporization of its water content leaves coagulated solids in milk, which is khoa. 175–180°F (about 80°C) is ideal temperature to avoid boiling and to minimize scorching.

Other quick way of making khoa is to continue mixing full fat milk powder to skimmed milk until it becomes khoa.

Varieties of Khoa:

There are three distinct varieties of khoa. They differ in their composition, body and textural characteristics and end use.

Pindi or batti – This variety is identified as a circular ball of hemispherical pat with compact mass, homogenous and smooth texture. It shall not show any sign of fat leakage or presence of free water. It possesses pleasant cooked flavour and devoid of objectionable tastes like burnt, acidic, etc. This variety of khoa is used in the manufacture of burfi, peda and other varieties of sweets.

Dhap or chikna – It is a raw (katcha) khoa characterized by loose but smooth texture and soft grains and sticky body. Dhap variety carries highest percentage of moisture over other varieties of khoa. This high moisture is necessary to provide adequate free water for soaking of maida (refined wheat flour) and semolina (suji) and for homogenous distribution of other ingredients in the preparation of smooth gulabjamun balls. This variety of khoa is used in the manufacture of gulabjamun, kalajamun, pantooa, carrot halwa, etc.

Danedar – This is characterized by the granular texture with hard grains of different sizes and shapes embedded in viscous serum. Slightly sour milk is preferred in the manufacture of this variety as it yields granular texture. This variety of khoa is used in the manufacture of kalakand, milk cake, etc.

Spoilage of Khoa:

Due to higher nutrients and high water content, Khoa is easily susceptible to growth of bacteria. Staphylococcus aureus and Bacillus cereus are the main contaminating micro organisms in khoa and they cause many food–borne diseases. Rancidity is one of the reasons which deteriorate quality of khoa and it adversely affects storage life of khoa. Addition of potassium sorbate effectively improves the storage life of khoa at higher temperatures.

Storage of khoa –

- Khoa should always be stored in cool dark place and away from any pungent smelling item.
- The storage life of khoa is only two to three days, under ambient conditions, and 15 –20 days under refrigerated conditions (5 –10℃).
- Increased storage stability of khoa for 40 days can be achieved by addition of potassium sorbate.

CHAPTER VII

YEAST

Yeast is an egg –shaped single –cell fungus that is only visible with a microscope. It takes 20,000,000,000 (twenty billion) yeast cells to weigh one gram. Yeast is the heart of the bread –making process. It's the essential ingredient that makes the dough rise and gives home –baked bread its wonderful taste and aroma.

Other ingredients are added to complete the reactions that result in a perfectly baked loaf of hot, crusty homemade bread. There are innumerable varieties of yeast. Of these, only a few are suited to bread. Saccharomyces cerevisiae, which means "sugar eating yeast". Strains of such yeast are isolated and then nurtured under simulated conditions. It is a biologically raising agent and its function is to make the dough rise in volume. It is during the rising and proving that carbon dioxide (CO2) is emitted and forms bubbles which not only cause the dough to rise, but make the baked bread porous, improves the grain, compressed and sold fresh or dried and sold in granular form. Yeast conditions the dough (gluten) so that it attains sufficient mellowness to stretch under the pressure of CO2 gas and form the structure of the products. The small quantity of alcohol produced evaporates in the heat of the oven.

Functions of Yeast in Bakery:

Yeast fermentation happens when the yeast cells "eat" sugar, the food of choice for yeast. Yeast fermentation in dough has **three** functions in bread making –

Rising the dough – yeast fermentation makes carbon dioxide, a gas responsible for stretching and expanding the dough like a balloon.

Dough development – other compounds formed during yeast fermentation make the flour stronger so it can capture and hold the carbon dioxide gas that the yeast produces.

Flavor, aroma and texture – yeast fermentation also provides these wonderful sensory and physical attributes that you expect from yeast –raised products.

How does yeast make bread rise? As bread dough is mixed and kneaded, millions of air bubbles are trapped and dispersed throughout the dough. Meanwhile under favourable moisture, warmth and pH, the yeast in the dough metabolizes the starches and sugars in the flour and starts to multiply. While multiplying, they excrete alcohol and carbon dioxide gas. The more the multiplication, the more will be the quantity of alcohol and carbondioxide. This gas inflates the network of air bubbles, causing the bread to rise. During rising, the yeast divides and multiplies, producing more alcohol and carbon dioxide. As long as there is ample air and food (carbohydrates) in the dough, the yeast will multiply until its activity is stopped by the oven's heat. During baking process the alcohol and carbon dioxide escapes with the vapour due to heat.

Yeast reproduction and multiplication:

Yeast cells reproduce and multiply under favourable conditions like –

• Sugar – Yeast feed upon the sugar, thus multiply through the process of fermentation. Sufficient sugar (up to 10%, average 6 –8%) must be added to facilitate proper fermentation.

• Warmth – 25 –400C

• Moisture – 80%

• Correct pH value of the ingredients – 4.5

The moisture is obtained from the liquid we use (water, milk, etc.). If the water used for making bread contains more salt (base), the growth is retarded. For the growth of yeast the food is available from the starch in flour or in the sugar added or by the addition of mineral yeast food (MYF). The warmth is obtained from the ingredients kept at room temperature. Addition of acid (eg.acetic acid) is recommended in the formula to correct the pH value to 4.5.

Types of Yeast:

There are two types of yeast–

• Fresh Yeast

• Dried Yeast

A. Fresh yeast: Fresh yeast is also known as compressed yeast or cake yeast. It is a moist mixture of yeast plants and starch. It should be kept in the refrigerator and should be maintained at 40 –450 F. It has a pleasant aroma like ripe apples and is inactive at cool temperature, yellowish cream in colour and when broken, it shows clean fracture without crumbling. It produces gas rapidly when added to dough. Bakers prefer fresh yeast because it is cheaper and reliable. It can be stored for 2 –4 weeks as it contains high moisture content.

Fresh yeast is divided into two –

• **Cream yeast** – Cream yeast is not available in Indian markets. This yeast is available in the suspension form and is transported by motor and tube. It can be stored only for 7 –10 days as it contains very high moisture content.

• **Compressed yeast** – is essentially cream yeast with most of the liquid removed. It is soft solid, beige in color, crumbly in appearance, and arguably best known in the consumer form as small, foil –wrapped cubes of cake yeast.

B. Dry yeast – contains very less moisture and has a good shelf life. It is grayish brown in colour and granular in form with a distinctive smell.

• **Active dry yeast** – It is a mixture of yeast with corn flour or corn meal pressed into cakes and dried. It is available in granular or and multiply. It with some growth medium. Under most conditions, active dry yeast must first be proofed or rehydrated is suitable for the sponge and dough methods. It can be stored for a long time (4 –6 months) due to less moisture content.

• **Instant dry yeast** – is the form of yeast most commonly available to noncommercial bakers. It consists of coarse oblong granules powder form. It continues to live but in an inactive stage. When it gets warmth and moisture it begins to develop of yeast, with live yeast cells encapsulated in a thick jacket of dry, dead cells. It can be stored at room temperature for a year, or frozen for more than a decade, which means that it has better keeping qualities than other forms, but it is generally considered more sensitive than other forms to thermal shock when actually used in recipes.

• **Rapid –rise yeast** – is a variety of dried yeast (usually a form of instant yeast) that is of a smaller granular size, thus it dissolves faster in dough, and it provides greater carbon dioxide output to allow faster rising. This yeast is not generally used in bakery as most baking experts believe it reduces the flavor potential of the finished product.

• **Deactivated yeast** – is dead yeast which has no leavening value and is not interchangeable with other yeast types. Typically used for pizza and pan bread doughs, it is used at a rate of 0.1% of the flour weight, though manufacturer specifications may vary. It is a powerful reducing agent used to increase the extensibility of dough.

Preparing yeast for dough:

Yeast can be added directly to dry ingredients.

• Use liquid temperatures of 120°F to 130°F for dry yeast.

• Use liquid temperatures of 90°F – 95°F for cake yeast.

OR, Yeast can be dissolved in liquids before mixing with the rest of the dry ingredients.

• Rehydrating dry yeast before using gives it a "good start" – the yeast feeds on the sugar allowing it to become very active and ready to work in your dough.

• Water is recommended for dissolving yeast.

• Dissolve 1 tsp sugar in ½ cup 110°F –115°F water.

• Add up to 3 packets of yeast, depending on your recipe, to the sugar solution.

• Stir in yeast until completely dissolved.

• Let mixture stand until yeast begins to foam vigorously (5 – 10 minutes).

• Add mixture to remaining ingredients.

• Remember to decrease the total liquids in your recipe by ½ cup to adjust for the liquid used to dissolve the yeast.

Important tips:

• Salt controls the yeast activity during fermentation and it has a tightening action on flour protein. So if the formula contains more salt, it reduces the yeast activity.

- If the sugar is concentrated, it will be difficult for the yeast to take food from it. If sugar is increased.
- Yeast should be slightly reduced if baking at high altitude.
- Milk and egg protein have a tightening action on flour proteins. In their presence the yeast function will be difficult and so more yeast will be necessary.
- During winter, yeast content should be increased.
- During summer, yeast content should be reduced to prevent souring of dough.
- If dough requires long fermentation period to develop flavor in bread, then one should reduce the yeast content.
- If dough requires fast fermentation, the quantity of yeast should be increased to make the dough light and spongy.
- If formula contains baking powder the quantity of yeast should be reduced.
- Using a thermometer is the most accurate way to determine the correct liquid temperature. Any thermometer will work as long as it measures temperatures between 75°F and 130°F.

Yeast culture:

A culture would be started by leaving a rye dough to stand at 24–27oC for several hours, which is likely to induce the grain microorganisms to start a lactic acid fermentation. An alternative is to add sour milk to the dough followed by resting the dough for a few hours. A mixture of pure organic acids can be added to simulate the flavour of proper sour dough. If the culture is to provide both the yeast and the flavour of sour dough then either it must acquire wild yeast or a starter culture that includes yeast must be added.

In some cases the sour dough culture is only used to give the sour dough taste while conventional yeast is added. If a started culture is used the culture is activated by mixing it with rye flour and water and leaving it to stand in a warm place until the culture is fully active. The active culture is then kept going by feeding it flour and water. When the culture is fully active the culture is mixed in with flour, water, salt and any fat. The resulting dough is kneaded carefully to avoid too much toughening. The dough is then fermented say for half to one hour, knocked back, scaled, proved and baked.

Some sour dough bread is made by using commercial yeast but with a proportion of genuine sour dough. Ordinary baker's yeast is at a disadvantage in rye sour dough because the low pH that is essential for rye bread is not the optimum pH for the yeast. Conventional improvers are not used in rye bread but additives are sometimes used to increase the water absorption of the dough. Examples are polysaccharide gums such as guar and locust bean gum as well as pre –gelatinized potato flour, rice starch or maize starch.

Storage of Yeast :

Yeast has three enemies –

- Air
- Moisture
- Heat

Excess of moisture, heat and air will retard in multiplication of yeast and also kills them. Dead yeast does not work on bread doughs, so extra precaution has to be observed while storing yeast.

• Unopened pack should be kept in clean, dry and cool place. In cool climate, they can be kept on shelves or cupboards. Where as in hot climate, they should be kept in refrigerator. Unopened, yeast will last about 2 years from the date of manufacture.

• Opened pack should be kept in airtight containers. It is preferable to purchase small packs, so that they can be used at one time.

• Never put damped spoon or finger into the yeast container. This type of yeast may last for 4 –5 months from the date of manufacture.

CHAPTER VIII

CHEMICAL LEAVENING AGENTS

Chemical leavening is a mechanism used in the baking industry to provide volume through the release of gases to enhance the eating quality of baked goods. Chemical leavening agents added to doughs and batters undergo various decomposition and neutralization reactions to produce carbon dioxide, water vapor and in some cases ammonia. These gases are responsible for expansion, flavor, color and other aesthetic aspects of baked products, namely crumb grain size, tenderness, etc. Chemical leaveners are used in quick breads and cakes.

Some common chemical agents include –

1. Baking Powder
2. Baking soda (Sodium Bicarbonate)
3. Cream of tartare
4. Ammonium Bicarbonate (Hartshorn, Horn Salt, Bakers Ammonia)
5. Potassium Bicarbonate (Potash or pearl ash)
6. Monocalcium phosphate monhydrate

1. Baking powder:

Baking powder is a dry chemical leavening agent used in baking. There are several formulations; all contain an alkali, typically sodium bicarbonate (baking soda), and an acid in the form of salt crystals, together with starch to keep it dry. It usually reacts in the presence of any acidic medium such as sour milk butter milk or orange juice, which causes carbon dioxide gas to release causing the desired result in baked goods. Mainly used in a variety of dishes such as biscuits batters pudding, etc. Baking powder is usually a single acting agent, which means it reacts as soon as it comes into contact with any liquid. Hence, it is extremely important to work quickly once milk or water comes into contact with the dry ingredients so that the resulting carbon dioxide does not get a chance to escape.

"*NaHCO3 +H+ (from the acid) → Na + H2O + CO2*"

2. Baking soda:

It is also known as Sodium bicarbonate NaHCO3 or sodium hydrogen carbonate, or bread soda, or bicarbonate of soda, which is a soluble white chemical compound, with a slight alkaline taste resembling that of sodium carbonate. It is found in many mineral springs and also produced artificially. Baking soda can be used either on its own or combined with an acid like cream of tartar to produce baking powder. Sodium bicarbonate can only be used without acid in systems in which the baking soda reaches a high enough temperature (>1201C) to decompose thermally –

"*2NaHCO3 + heat → Na2CO3 + Co2 + H2O*"

The reaction with acids is:

"*2NaHCO3 + heat+ → Na++CO2 + H2O*"

Sodium bicarbonate is soluble in water at 01C; a saturated solution is 6.5% with the solubility rising to 14.7% at 601C. It can be expected then that sodium bicarbonate will dissolve in the aqueous phase of a batter or dough. It will then react with any acid present, including any acid ingredients such as butter milk.

3. Cream of tartar:

Cream of tartar is fine white powder which is extracted from the
tartaric acid that crystallizes in wine casks during the fermentation process of grapes. It is
also known as potassium salt and has a number of uses. It may be combined with
bicarbonate of soda to produce baking powder it can also be added to increase stability and
volume of whisked egg whites to increase their stability when making meringues or folded
into cake batters. Adding a small amount to sugar syrups will prevent it from crystallizing
and hence used in sugar work and decorations.

4. Ammonium Bicarbonate:

Commercial ammonium bicarbonate was formerly known as salt volatile or salt of hartshorn or bakers ammonia and was formerly obtained by the dry distillation of nitrogenous organic matter such as hair, horn, decomposed urine, etc., but is now obtained by heating a mixture ammoniumcarbonate, ammonium bicarbonate, and ammonium carba –mate. Ammonium bicarbonate is used in the food industry as a raising agent for flat baked goods, such as cookies, crackers, steamed buns and cookies. It was commonly used in the home before modern day baking powder was made available to home bakers. It decomposes rapidly during baking to form carbon dioxide gas, ammonia gas, and water. Only heat and moisture are necessary for it to work.

No acids are needed. Compared to baking soda or potash, hartshorn has the advantage of producing more gas for the same amount of agent, and of not leaving any

salty or soapy taste in the finished product, as it completely decomposes into water and gaseous products which evaporate during baking. It cannot be used for moist, bulky baked goods however, such as normal bread or cakes, since some ammonia will be trapped inside and will cause an unpleasant taste. It is stable at room temperature, but decomposes 401C, i.e. in the
early stages of the oven. The reaction for the decomposition is –

"*NH4CO3 → NH3 + CO2 + H2O*"

5. Potassium bi –carbonate:

Potassium bicarbonate (also known as potassium hydrogen carbonate or potassium acid carbonate), is a colorless, odorless, slightly basic, salty substance. The compound is used as a source of carbon dioxide for leavening in baking. It is used as a base in foods to regulate pH. It is a common ingredient in club soda, where it is used to soften the effect of effervescence. This is also known as pearl ash or Potash. It is KHCO3 which causes leavening in a baked product. This is sometimes used to make gingerbreads, biscuits and honey cakes. Potassium bicarbonate is also more expensive. The reaction for its thermal decomposition is –

"*2KHCO3 + heat → K2CO3 + CO2 + H2O*"

6. Monocalcium phosphate dehydrate:

The most important use of the monocalcium phosphate in the food industry is as the acid component in the baking powders. It has application in foods such as Pancakes, cookies, angel food cakes, self –rising flour, double acting baking powder and single acting baking powder.Once it is combined with sodium bicarbonate or another alkali, it will produce carbon dioxide, It is a low temperature acid, which will react immediately as moisture is added. It also works as a pH regulator in the baked product, due to the resulting buffer salts from the fermentation process.

Other chemical leaveners used may be –

1. Dicalcium phosphate dihydrate (CPD)
2. Sodium aluminum sulfate (SAS)
3. Anhydrous monocalcium phosphate (AMCP)
4. Sodium aluminum phosphate (SALP)
5. Sodium acid pyrophosphate (SAPP)
6. Tartaric acid
7. Glucono –delta –lactone
8. Calcium sulfate
9. Calcium carbonate

Storage of Chemical Leaveners:

All chemical leaveners have a shelf life upto 3 years if stored properly. They should be kept tightly closed air proof containers. If left open, they can absorb moisture from the air and lose part of their leavening power. Also, they must be stored in a cool and dark place, because heat also causes them to deteriorate due to oxidation.

CHAPTER IX

SALT

These are chemical compound (other than water) formed by a chemical reaction between an acid and a base. Salt for human consumption is produced in different form sun refined salt (such as sea salt), refined salt (table salt), and iodized salt. It is a crystalline solid, white, pale pink or light gray in color, normally obtained from sea water or rock deposits.

Edible rock salts may be slightly grayish in color because of mineral content. It is essential for animal life in small quantities, but is harmful to animals and plants in excess. Salt is one of the oldest, most ubiquitous food seasonings and salting is an important method of food preservation. The taste of salt (saltiness) is one of the basic human tastes.

Classification of salt –

1. Table salt – Once of the most widely used salts, table salt goes through a refining process that removes traces of other naturally occurring minerals. Chemical additives such as sodium silicoaluminate, calcium phosphate, or magnesium carbonate are sometimes blended in to prevent clumping. Table salt and iodized salt are preferred in baking for their fine –grained texture and accuracy of measure.

2. Iodized salt – A form of table salt, iodized salt is fortified with iodine that was lost during processing. Iodized salt was the first functional food, fortified in the early 1920s in response to a Midwest –focused epidemic of goiter (hyperthyroidism) that was caused by iodine deficiencies.

3. Kosher salt – This inexpensive coarse salt is evaporated from a brine, usually under specific conditions approved by the Orthodox Jewish faith. It contains no additives or added iodine. It has a much larger grain size than some common table salt. Like common table salt, kosher salt consists of the chemical compound sodium chloride. Kosher salt typically contains no additives (for example, iodide), although some brands will include anti –clumping agents in small amounts. Additive –free non – kosher salt is also readily available and is generally preferred in professional kitchens due to its ease of being measured by hand.

4. Sea salt – Available in, fine and coarse grains, sea salt has become increasingly available in markets but at a higher cost than table or kosher salt. Sea salt is made from evaporated sea water. Some salt farmers evaporate the water in enclosed bays along the shoreline, and then rake up the salt by hand. This type of salt tends to include several naturally present trace minerals, such as iodine, magnesium, and potassium, which give sea salt a fresher, lighter flavor than standard table salt. These are best used where their tremendous flavor and presence is pronounced, such as on a boiled potato or a slice of tomato.

5. Rock salt– Sold in large crystals, rock salt has a grayish hue because it is unrefined. Rock salt makes a great bed for serving oysters and clams. Or combine it with ice to make ice cream in hand –cranked ice cream makers.

6. Black salt or kalanamak or black Indian salt – is a salty and pungent smelling condiment used in India. The condiment is composed largely of sodium chloride with several impurities lending the salt its colour and smell. The smell is mainly due to sulfur content.

7. Smoked salt – is an aromatic edible salt product with smoke flavoring. It is a seasoning and is used as a shortcut to add smoked flavor to foods. Smoked salt consists mainly of sea salt and smoke volatiles condensed on the salt. An ingredient typically listed on smoked salt is sawdust.

Uses of salt in bakery –

1. Acts as preservative, as it acts on microorganisms, extracts the liquid from them and then kills them.

2. Acts as anti –raising agent – regulates the leavening processes in breads by controlling the action of yeast.

3. Salt slows down all the chemical reactions that are happening in the dough, including calming fermentation activity to a steadier level.

4. Salt also makes the dough a little stronger strengthening effect on the gluten protein in the dough.

5. Salt adds flavor to baked goodsand mask the off –flavours. It also potentiates the flavor of other ingredients, including butter and flour.

CHAPTER X

SPICES

Spices are used for flavour, colour, aroma and preservation of food or beverages. Spices may be derived from many parts of the plant– bark, buds, flowers, fruits, leaves, rhizomes, roots, seeds, stigmas and styles or the entire plant tops. The term 'herb' is used as a subset of spice and refers to plants with aromatic leaves. The characteristics and environmental needs of the crops dominating the global spice trade are described below.

> *"Spices are often dried and used in a processed but complete state. Another option is to prepare extracts such as essential oils by distilling the raw spice material (wet or dry), or to use solvents to extract oleoresins and other standardized products. Coriander, cumin, mustard, and sesame seeds and the herbs sage, oregano, thyme, bay and the mints are the most important spice crops from non –tropical environments."*

Allspice– Allspice (also known as English Spice, English Pepper, Jamaica pepper, Clove Pepper, Myrtle pepper, Pimenta, Pimento, or Newspice) is a Caribbean spice discovered by Christopher Columbus on the island of Jamaica during his second voyage of 1493–1496 CE. The spice itself is the dried, unripe, (green) fruit of the Pimentadioica plant which is a small shrubby tree, quite similar to the bay laurel in size and form and a member of the Myrtaceae (Myrtle) family.The English name 'allspice' was coined in England by 1621 and is derived from the English belief that this spice combined the flavour of several spices– most notable cloves, pepper, cinnamon and nutmeg. It is also an ingredient in commercial sausage preparations and in many curry powders and barbecue sauces. It is also a common ingredientof British cooking where it is often used to lift the flavour of many dishes (especially cakes).

Aniseeds– Aniseed (also known as Anise, Anís or Sweet Cumin) are the seed pods (fruit) of Pimpinellaanisum a herbacious flowering plant of the Apiaceae (also known as Umbelliferae) family of flowering plants. The plant is native to the eastern Mediterranean and southwest Asia and grows to 50cm tall. The plant is native to the eastern Mediterranean and southwest Asia and grows to 50cm tall. This is a very versatile spice with a rather heady aroma which explains its versatility. Aniseed is also believed to be a substance that enhances lactation. In the West (and the Middle East), aniseed is most typically used to flavoure breads, cakes and most especially biscuits (cookies) is also used in anise –flavored liqueurs (such as raki, arak and ouzo) and is the dominant ingredient used in absinthe.

Black peppercorn– Black pepper represents the dried fruit of the flowering vine, Piper nigruma member of the Piperaceae(pepper) family. The pepper vine is a native of south – western India and has been traded from there since prehistory. White pepper (image, bottom) in contrast is made from only the seed of the pepper fruit. The outer fruit wall is removed by allowing fully ripe berries to soak in water for about a week, during which time the flesh of the fruit softens and decomposes. Rubbing then removes what remains of the fruit, and the naked seed is dried. Pepper gains its spicy heat from the piperinecompound which is present both in the seed and the outer fruit (which is why most people believe white pepper to be milder than black pepper).Asian cooks tend to prefer white pepper to black pepper and the unique blend of pungency and aromatic overtones found in black pepper means that this spice marries with both savoury and sweet dishes.

Caraway seeds– Ajwain (also known as – Carom, Caraway, Ajowan, Bishop's Weed and Seeds Of Bishop's Weed) represent the seed –like fruit of the Bishop's Weed plant Trachyspermumammi. Carumcopticum, a member of the Apiaceae (parsley) family. It is primarily used in Indian cuisine, but is also used in dishes from Iran, Egypt, Ethiopia and Afghanistan. Raw ajwain smells almost exactly like thyme because it also contains thymol, but is more aromatic and less subtle in taste, as well as slightly bitter and musty. The heat being produced by capsaicin (8 –methyl –N –vanillyl –6 –nonenamide) and several related chemicals, collectively called capsaicinoids. They are used in preparation of vegetable fillers, breads and pies.

Cardamom– Cardamoms are members of the ginger family, theZingiberaceae and both the entire seed pods and the seeds themselves can be used as spice distinct yet overlapping sensory qualities. Cardamom is of two types– green and black. Although Indian green cardamom (sometimes known as 'True Cardamom') is by far the most familiar, there are in fact five related species, distributed from Africa to Australasia, that yield four separate and distinct spices, with. Cardamom can also be used to flavour milk in the generation of custards and cakes. Indeed, unlike all the other cardamoms described above, green cardamom is the only one used in both sweet and savory dishes. Ground cardamom is of much poorer quality, as the aromatic compounds that give cardamom its unique flavour are volatile and are lost quickly on grinding. It is always better to use freshly –ground cardamom. Although black cardamom (which is more robust in terms of flavour profile) tends to be used in spicier or more rustic dishes whereas green cardamom is used in more fragrant and subtly spiced dishes. Both spices have distinct places in cookery.

Cayenne– orChillies (also known as Chili, Chilé and Ají) are the fruit of the Capsicum members of the Solanaceae(deadly nightshade) family.They all originate in the Americas, where they have been cultivated for at least 7500 years.Chilli peppers add both flavour and 'heat' to a dish. . Indeed, the flavour is so strong that even a small amount can completely overwhelm the flavour of a dish. The spice is often added to Indian breads and is used as a flavouring to snack foods such as biscuits.

Celery seeds– Celery seeds are the fruit of the Celery plant, Apiumgraveolens, a herbaceous biennial plant in the family Apiaceae (Umbellifarae) a huge family that contains carrots, cumin, caraway and fennel.They add greatly to the flavour of potatoes and are especially potato salad. The seeds can also be used in buns, breads, salad dressings, sauces and gravies. However, celery seeds do have a strong celery –like flavour (and a slightly bitter aftertaste) and should be used sparingly so as not to overwhelm a dish.

Nigella – Nigella seeds (also known as Fennel flower, Nutmeg flower, Onion seed, Gith, Kalonji Seeds, blackseeds) are produced by the plant Nigella sativa — though there are about 14 species of Nigella in all, which are annual plants in the Ranunculaceae (buttercup) family; all native to southern Europe, north Africa and southwest The black seeds are small and sharp –edged and have a peppery, slightly nutty, taste and are generally used as a pepper substitute in recipes that incorporate pod fruit, vegetables, salads and poultry. Nigella flavoured breads, pies and buns are readily available in the bakes shop.

Cinnamon – Cinnamon (also known as Celylon Cinnamon) is the dried inner bark of Cinnamomumverum a small evergreen tree reaching about 15m tall and a member of the Lauraceae (laurel) family (which also includes Bay, Avocado and Sassafrass) which is a native of Sri Lanka and Southern India. The bark of the tree is sliced off and then let to dry.Cinnamon is generally used as flavouring for sweet foods such as cakes and desserts.

Cloves – Clove trees are members of the Myrtaceae (Myrtle) family. It is native to Indonesia and used as a spice in cuisine all over the world.The name derives from French clou, a nail, as the dried buds, which form the spice itself, vaguely resemble that makes this spice suitable for both sweet and savoury dishes and why it is frequently employed in aromatic small irregular medieval nails in shape. Cloves are unusual in that they combine an aromatic and floral fragrance (that can be a little medicinal) with a fiery and burning taste. It is this combination vegetable fillings and breads. The essential oil of cloves is dominated by eugenol (70 to 85%), eugenol acetate (15%) and β –caryophyllene (5 to 12%).

Coriander– Coriander (commonly called cilantro in North America) is the plant Coriandrumsativum which is an annual herb of the family Apiaceae (also known as Umbelliferae). As such it is a member of a huge family that contains carrots, cumin, caraway and fennel. Coriander is native to southwestern Asia west to North Africa. Ground coriander seeds are major component of most curry powders and are used as a flavouring ingredient in breads,fillings, and savoury mousses.

Cumin– As a spice Cumin (also known as White Cumin) is the dried fruit of the Cuminumcyminumplant which is a member of the Apiaceae (also known as Umbelliferae) family. It is therefore related to carrots, caraway and fennel and distantly related to Black Cumin. The plant is native to a region from the eastern Mediterranean through to India. Cumin is used as a spice for its distinctive aroma, and is popular in North African, Middle Eastern, western Chinese, Indian and Mexican cuisine.

Dill– Dill, Anethumgraveolens (also known as Dillby, King Desertparsley, Shepu or Sowa) is a short –lived annual herb that's a member of the Umbelliferae (carrot/parsley) family. Originally a native of southwest and central Asia it has been naturalized to much of the world due to its culinary uses. Like the herb, dill seeds are sweet and aromatic, with a flavour that is mildyaniseedy, coming somewhere between anise and caraway. The main component of the essential oil from the fruit is carvone and limonene. Plants in Europe and south –western Asia can grow to 2m tall. Dill is characteristic of central European cuisines, particularly Germany where they are used to flavour breads, salads and pickles. Apart from in India, the dill herb is much more popular than the spice.

Fennel– Fennel (also known as Sweet Cumin), Foeniculumvulgare is a species in the Apiaceae (also known as umbellifearae) family, which also includes carrots, cumin, caraway and fennel. It is an aromatic perennial herb, a native of southern Asia.The main component of the essential oil of fennel seeds is anethole (the oil also contains limonene, fenchone, estragole (methyl chavicol), safrole, α –pinene, camphene, β –pinene, β – myrcene and p –cymene, but to a much lesser degree). It is an essential ingredient in the Bengali spice mixture panchphoron and in Chinese five –spice powders. In the west, fennel seed is a very common ingredient in Italian sausages and northern European rye breads.

Fenugreek– Fenugreek, Trigonellafoenum –graecum has a native realm that extends from the eastern Mediterranean across to China, though it is now cultivated worldwide. This is an important element of many pickles, curry powders and pastes, and is often encountered in the cuisine of the Indian subcontinent and Thailand. The seeds are quite large (about 3mm), are brownish –yellow in colour and rhombic in form and have a bitter taste that mellows when cooked and a very distinctive 'curry –like' aroma which is created by the aromatic compound, sotolone . It is also used in Ethiopian spice mixtures (particularly Berbere spice), is particularly favoured in Yemeni cuisine and is used in the cuisines of West, Central and South Asia (which are now the largest consumers).

Garlic– Alliumsativum, commonly known as garlic, is a species in the onion genus, Allium. Its close relatives include the onion, shallot, leek, chive,andrakkyo.It is also used in Ethiopian spice mixtures (particularly Berbere spice), is particularly flavoured in Yemeni cuisine and is used in the cuisines of West, Central and South Asia (which are now the largest consumers). Garlic is a particularly pungent spice, though the pungency disappears after frying in oil (or baking for a lengthy period). The pungency and distinctive aroma of garlic is due to the large number of sulfur –containing compounds within each clove. Though typically cooked in Europe (exceptions being Aïoli and

Tzatzike), raw garlic is commonly used in the cuisines of India, Pakistan, Bangladesh, China and Vietnam. In Thailand, garlic is often fried until crisp and is then used to garnish dishes.

Ginger– Ginger, Zingiberofficinale is the archetypical member of the Zingiberaceae (ginger) family and though it is generally termed as 'ginger root' the spice is actually the rhizome of the plant. Originating in southern China, cultivation of ginger spread to India, juice from old ginger roots Southeast Asia, West Africa, and the Caribbean. Young ginger roots are juicy and fleshy with a very mild taste where as mature ginger roots are fibrous and nearly dry. The is extremely potent and is often used as a spice in Asian cuisine to cover up other strong odours and flavours such as in seafood and mutton. Ginger has been used in European cuisine since medieval times when it arrived as a dried spice and gave rise to Ginger Bread. Powdered ginger is extensively used in flavouring biscuits, pies, breads and mousse.

Juniper– The Common Juniper Juniperuscommunis is a large woody shrub and a member of the Cupressaceae (cypress) family of conifers. It is highly aromatic with found in sub – artic and temperate zones throughout the Northern Hemisphere and is knon in the Americas, Europe and Asia. The astringent blue –black seed cones, known colloquially as 'juniper berries' (they are actually cones or pseudofruit) are usually sold dried and used to flavour meats, sauces and stuffings. They are generally crushed before use to release their flavour. Juniper berries are a sweet slightly pine –like scent, though there is a marked bitter after –taste. These find their ways in preparation of a number of fillers, breads, jams, jellies etc.

Mace and Nutmeg– These both come from the evergreen tree species Myristicafragrans that originate only from the Banda Islands of Eastern Indonesia (the Moluccas). This tree is a member of the Myristicaceae (generally referred to as the Nutmeg) family. Nutmegs bear yellowish fruit with a white pulp (which is rather apricot –like) — see the image, below. This is split to reveal the seed inside. The seed itself is covered by'lacy' reddish covering (the arillus) and it is this arillus in dried form that yields mace. The seed within is the nutmeg. Both seed and arillus are generally sun –dried for about two months after which the arillus is removed and the seed itself is cracked, revealing the fragrant nutmeg interior. Both nutmeg and mace have similar taste qualities, though nutmeg is slightly sweeter in taste and mace has a more delicate flavour. Mace is more expensive and tends to be used in light –coloured dishes where it imparts a bright yellow saffron –like colour.

Marjoram– Marjoram (Origanummajorana, Lamiaceae) is a somewhat cold –sensitive perennial herb or under –shrub with sweet pine and citrus flavours. In some Middle – eastern countries, marjoram is synonymous with oregano, and there the names sweet marjoram and knotted marjoram are used to distinguish it from other plants of the genus Origanum. It is cultivated for its aromatic leaves, either green or dry, for culinary purposes. Marjoram is sweeter and milder than oregano. It is an important ingredient for German sausages, breads and savoury puddings.

Mustard–Mustard seeds are the seeds of several plant species (all related to rapeseed) that produce seeds which are used as a spice. They are members of the Brassica family that includes broccoli, cauliflower, cabbage, kale and Swedes. Once the cell is damaged (such as by crushing or grinding), the enzyme myrosinase hydrolyzes the sinalbin and produces free p –hydroxyl benzylisothiocyanate, a pungent and non –volatile substance. Mustards Indian recipes may be white ones, the brown ones and the black ones. White mustard in the native of North Africa, the Middle East and Mediterranean Europe and are grown for their seeds only. The dried seeds themselves do not have any taste, but exhibit a considerable pungency when crushed or ground and mixed with water (such as on chewing). Brown mustard is grown in the foothills of the Himalaya, UK, Canada and the US. This is an essential ingredient in many and has a higher level of volatile mustard oils that white mustard (and is thus stronger in taste and pungency, but not as strong as black mustard). Black mustard (Brassica nigra) is grown in Argentina, Chile, the US and some European countries. This has the highest concentration of volatile mustard oil of all the mustard seeds and is by far the most pungent variety.

Oregano– It is a common species of Origanum, a genus of the mint family (Lamiaceae). It is native to warm –temperate western and southwestern Eurasia and the Mediterranean region. Oregano's most prominent modern use is as the staple herb of Italian –American cuisine. Oregano's most prominent modern use is as the staple herb of Italian –American cuisine. It is also popularly used in making vegetables fillers and breads.

Poppy seeds– Poppy Seeds are the seeds of the annual plant Papaversomniferum (the opium poppy), a member of the Ranunculales (buttercup) family. This is a very ancient spice, known to have been cultivated for at last 5000 years and there is some indication that the culinary use of poppy seeds extends much further back in time (the seeds have been found in many ancient burials). Poppy seeds have a pleasant and nutty flavour, which intensifies upon baking (which is why poppy seeds are used as a topping for many baked goods). Interestingly, poppy seeds are a good source of linolenic acid, which is an essential compound in the human diet. It is used profoundly in making cakes, breads, strudels etc.

Rosemary– Rosemary, Rosmarinusofficinalis, is a woody, perennial herb with fragrant, evergreen, needle –like leaves and white, pink, purple or blue flowers, native to the Mediterranean region and is a member of the mint family Lamiaceae, The leaves, both fresh and dried, are used in traditional Mediterranean cuisine. They have a bitter, astringent taste and are highly aromatic, which complements a wide variety of foods.

Saffron– Saffron is a spice derived from the saffron crocus Crocussativus, members of the Iridaceae (Iris) family. The flower itself has three red stigmas (right –hand image) that are the distal ends of the plant's carpels. Together with its style (the stalk that connects the stigmas to the remainder of the plant) these components are often dried and used in cooking as a seasoning and colouring agent. Saffron is native to Southwestern Asia, Saffron's aroma is often described by connoisseurs as reminiscent of metallic honey with grassy, while its taste has been noted also as hay –like and yet somewhat bitter. Saffron also contributes a luminous yellow –orange colouring to foods. Because of the unusual taste and colouring it adds to foods, saffron is widely used in Arab, Central Asian, European, Indian, Iranian, and Moroccan cuisines

Sesame– Sesame seeds (also known as Gingelly and Benneseed) are the seeds of the sesame plant Sesamumindicum, and being the plant's seeds they are classed as a spice. Indeed, they are the oldest spice known from written human records and figure in an Assyrian myth circa 3000 BCE. Sesame seeds can range in colour from off –white through brown to black. The seeds have a nutty flavour and are distinctly oily when chewed. The nutty taste is significantly increased by toasting (which is why sesame seeds are often used as toppings for breads and cakes)

Star anis– Star Anise is the star –shaped pericarp (the outer part of a fruit, excluding the seeds) of lliciumverum, a small native evergreen tree of southwest China. The dried fruit resembles an eight –pointed star and has a flavour that closely resembles that of anise (hence the English and Chinese names). It forms on of the key components of Chinese five spice powder. It can be used as cheaper version of aniseed.

Turmeric– Turmeric (also Tumeric, Indian Saffron or Kunyit) is a spice formed from the rhizome of Curcuma longa, a representative of plant genus Curcuma and a member of the ginger family, the Zingiberaceae. The most common form of turmeric is the dried and powdered rhizome which is commonly used in curries and other South Asian cuisine and is a significant ingredient in most commercial curry powders. Turmeric is often used as a yellow colourant in food and is a crucial component in many curries.

CHAPTER XI

FLAVOURINGS

"There is a good deal of evidence that the sensory characteristics of food, in particular the taste and flavour have a very specific effect on the consumer's food choice. In many ways the sensory attributes could be seen as a key area in which food manufacturers can differentiate their products. These elements add sensory impressions of the food added with. They play a vital role on the characteristic of the cooked products and their patability, nutrition, aroma and taste. There are numerous taste enhancers used in food industry to meet the choice of requirement by the consumers."

Flavor or flavour (see spelling differences) is the sensory impression of a food or other substance, and is determined mainly by the chemical senses of taste and smell. The flavor of the food, as such, can be altered with natural or artificial flavorants, which affect these senses. Flavorant is defined as a substance that gives another substance flavor, altering the characteristics of the solute, causing it to become sweet, sour, tangy, etc. Of the three chemical senses, smell is the main determinant of a food item's flavor. While the taste of food is limited to sweet, sour, bitter, salty, and savory – the basic tastes – the smells of a food are potentially limitless. A food's flavor, therefore, can be easily altered by changing its smell while keeping its taste similar. Nowhere is this better exemplified than in artificially flavored jellies, soft drinks and candies, which, while made of bases with a similar taste, have dramatically different flavors due to the use of different scents or fragrances.

Although the terms "flavoring" or "flavorant" in common language denote the combined chemical sensations of taste and smell, the same terms are usually used in the fragrance and flavors industry to refer to edible chemicals and extracts that alter the flavor of food and food products through the sense of smell. Due to the high cost or unavailability of natural flavor extracts, most commercial flavorants are nature –identical, which means that they are the chemical equivalent of natural flavors but chemically synthesized rather than being extracted from the source materials.

Flavoring agents –

Flavoring agents are the largest single group of food additives. Food and beverage applications of flavors include dairy, fruit, nut, seafood, spice blends, vegetables and wine flavoring agents. They may complement, magnify, or modify the taste and aroma of the foods. There are over 1200 different flavoring agents used in foods to create flavor or replenish flavors lost or diminished in processing, and hundreds of chemicals may be used to simulate nature flavors.

Classification of flavouring agents –

1. Natural flavoring agents – Natural materials include spices and herbs; essential oils and their extracts, concentrates, and isolates; fruit, fruit juices, and fruit essence; animal and vegetable materials and their extracts;

and aromatic chemicals isolated by physical means from natural products, eg. citral from lemongrass and linalool from bois de rose, extraction from certain plant products such as vanilla beans, licorice root, orange and lemon peel, coffee, tea, kola nuts, catechu, cherry, elm bark, cocoa nibs, and gentian root.

2. Nature identical flavoring substances – Flavoring substances that are obtained by synthesis or isolated through chemical processes, which are chemically identical to flavoring substances naturally present in products intended for human consumption. They cannot contain any artificial flavoring substances.Nature identical flavouring substances include– ethyl acetate (identical in nature to many fruits) and decanal (nature identical to orange). Vanillin may be obtained from vanilla pods but the flavour is now produced chemically from a plant material called lignin.

3. Artificial flavoring agents – Synthetic flavoring agents are chemically similar to natural flavorings, and offer increased consistency in use and availability. They may be less expensive and more readily available than the natural counterpart although they may not adequately simulate the natural flavor.

Some examples of synthetic flavoring agents include the following: –

- Almond – 5 –methylthiophen –2 –carboxaldehyde, benzaldehyde
- Anise – anethole, methyl chavicol (estragol)
- Apple – isoamyl acetate ,ethyl 2 –methylbutyrate, damaseneone, n – hexanal,trans –2 –hexenal

- Banana – isoamyl acetate
- Butter – diacetyl
- Caramel – 2,5 –dimethyl –4 –hydroxy –3(2h)furanone
- Caraway – d –carvone
- Celery – 3 –propylidene –1(3h) –isobenzofuranone, cis –3 –hexenyl pyruvate
- Cherry – benzaldehyde,tolylaldehyde,benzyl acetate
- Chocolate – 5 –methyl –2 –phenyl –2 –hexenal,isoamyl butyrate,vanillin, ethyl vanillin,isoamylphenylacetate, 2 –methoxy –5 –methylpyrazine
- Cinnamon – cinnamic aldehyde
- Coconut – g –nonalactone
- Coffee – furfurylmercaptan, furfurylthiopropionate
- Clove – eugenol
- Coriander – linalool
- Cream – cis –4 –heptenal
- Cucumber – nona –trans –2 –cis –6 –dienal, 2 –nonenal
- Garlic – methyl anthranilate, ethyl 3 –hydroxybutyrate, nootkatone
- Hazelnut – methyl(methylthio) pyrazine,5 –methyl –2 –hepten –4 –one
- Lemon – citral
- Maple – 2 –hydroxy –3 –methyl –2 –cyclopenten –1 –one
- Mint – menthol
- Mustard – allylisothiocyanate
- Orange – b –sinensal, octyl aldehyde, decyl aldehyde
- Peanut – 2,5 –dimethylpyrazine,2 –methoxy –5 –methylpyrazine
- Pineapple – allylcaproate, methyl b –methylthiopropionate, ethyl butyrate,allylcyclohexanpropionate

- Raspberry – 6 –methyl –a –ionone,trans –a –ionone,p –hydroxypheny –1 –2 –butanone,damasceneone
- Strawberry – ethylmethylphenylglycidate, ethyl maltol, methyl cinnamate,4 –hydroxy –2,5 –dimethyl –3(2h) –furanone
- Vanilla – vanillin, ethyl vanillin, propenylquaethol

CHAPTER XII

COCOA AND CHOCOLATE

Cocoa is the dried and fully fermented fatty seed of the cacao tree, from which cocoa solids and cocoa butter are extracted. They are the basis of chocolate.

The cacao tree (*Theobroma cacao*) is native of warm and humid climates around the equator. It is s a small (48 m or 1526 ft tall) evergreen tree in the family. It may have originated in

the foothills of the Andes in the Amazon and Orinoco basins of South America where today, examples of wild cacao still can be found. Cacao trees w ll grow in a limited geographical zone, of approximately 2 degrees to the north and south of the Equator. Nearly 70% of the world crop is grown in West Africa. A tree begns to bear when it is four or five years old. A mature tree may have 6,00 flowers in a year, yet only about 2pods. About 300 –60 seeds (1pods) are required to produce 1 kg (2.2 lb) of cocoa paste.

Varieties of Cocoa :

Cocoa can be classified into 4 types –

- ***Forastero*** – forms the greater part of all cocoa grown, is hardy and vigorous producing beans with the strongest and more bitter flavour flavor and is usually blended with other varieties.

- ***Amelonado*** –is the Forastero variety most widely grown in West Africa and Brazil. It has a smooth yellow pod with 3 or more pale to deep purple beans.

- ***Crillo*** –with its mild chocolate flavour is grown in Indonesia, Central and South America. Crillo trees are not as hardy and they produce softer and fragile pods which are red in colour, containing 20 –30 white, ivory or very pale purple beans.

- ***Trinitario*** –plants are not found in the wild as they are cultivated hybrids of the other two types (crillo and forastero). Trinitario cocoa trees are grown mainly in the Caribbean area but also in Cameroon and Papua New Guinea. The mostly hard pods are variable in colour and they contain 3or more beans of variable colour but white beans are rare.

Processing:

The harvested pods are opened typically with a curved knife the pulp and cocoa seeds are removed and the rind is discarded. The pulp and seeds are then piled in heaps, placed in bins, or laid out on grates for several days. During this time, the seeds and pulp undergo sweating, where the thick pulp liquefies as it ferments. The fermented pulp trickles away, leaving cocoa seeds behind to be collected. Sweating is important for the quality of the beans, which originally have a strong bitter taste. The fermented beans are dried by spreading them out over a large surface and constantly raking them which can be done on huge trays under the sun or by using artificial heat. Finally, the beans are trodden and shuffled about (often using bare human feet) and sometimes, during this process, red clay mixed with water is sprinkled over the beans to obtain a finer color, polish, and protection against molds during shipment to factories.

Chocolate production : Chocolate is a range of products derived from cocoa (cacao), mixed with fat (i.e. cocoa butter and / or plant oils) and finely powdered sugar to produce a solid confection. There are several types according to the proportion of cocoa used in a particular formulation.

To make 1 kg (2.2 pounds) of chocolate, about 30 to 60 healthy beans are processed, depending on the desired cocoa content. In a factory, the beans are roasted and then cracked and de –shelled by a winnower. The resulting pieces of beans are called *nibs,* which are ground, using various methods where the heat produced during this procedure melts the cocoa butter releasing *chocolate liquor or cocoa paste*, which is removed by being pressed out. This liquoris then further processed into chocolate by mixing in (more) cocoa butter and sugar (and sometimes vanilla and lecithin as an emulsifier), and then refined, *conched* and tempered. The cocoa solids will now be formed into a dry cake and used as the base ingredient in the production of chocolate or processed into a fine cocoa powder using a hydraulic press or the *Broma* process. This process produces around 50% cocoa butter and 50% cocoa powder. Standard cocoa powder has a fat content of approximately 10 –12 %.

Process of Transforming Cocoa beans into Chocolate:

Step 1. The cocoa beans are cleaned to remove all extraneous material.

Step 2. To bring out the chocolate flavour and colour the beans are roasted. The temperature, time and degree of moisture involved in roasting depend on the type of beans used and the sort of chocolate or product required from the process.

Step 3. A winnowing machine is used to remove the shells from the beans to leave just the cocoa nibs.

Step 4. The cocoa nibs undergo alkalisation, usually with potassium carbonate, to develop the flavour and colour.

Step 5. The nibs are then milled to create cocoa liquor (cocoa particles suspended in cocoa butter). The temperature and degree of milling varies according to the type of nib used and the product required.

Step 6. Manufacturers generally use more than one type of bean in their products and therefore the different beans have to be blended together to the required formula.

Step 7. The cocoa liquor is pressed to extract the cocoa butter leaving a solid mass called cocoa presscake. The amount of butter extracted from the liquor is controlled by the manufacturer to produce presscake with different proportions of fat.

Step 8. The processing now takes two different directions. The cocoa butter is used in the manufacture of chocolate. The cocoa presscake is broken into small pieces to form kibbled presscake which is then pulverized to form cocoa powder.

Step 9. Cocoa liquor is used to produce chocolate through the addition of cocoa butter. Other ingredients such as sugar, milk, emulsifying agents and cocoa butter equivalents are also added and mixed. The proportions of the different ingredients depends on the type of chocolate being made.

Step 10. The mixture then undergoes a refining process by travelling through a series of rollers until a smooth paste is formed. Refining improves the texture of the chocolate.

Step 11. The next process, conching, further develops flavour and texture. Conching is a kneading or smoothing process. The speed, duration and temperature of the kneading affect the flavour. An alternative to conching is an emulsifying process using a machine that works like an egg beater.

Step 12. The mixture is then tempered or passed through a heating, cooling and reheating process. This prevents discolouration and fat bloom in the product by preventing certain crystalline formations of cocoa butter developing.

Step 13. The mixture is then put into moulds or used for enrobing fillings and cooled in a cooling chamber.

Step 14. The chocolate is then packaged for distribution to retail outlets

Cocoa producing countries of the world:

Conching – here the cocoa solids are mixed together with cocoa butter slowly for few days, when they develop a smooth subtle texture and flavour. Then it is fortified with other ingredients like cocoa butter, sugar, vanilla, soya lethicinetc to impart a particular texture and taste.

Types of Cocoa powders – There are two types of cocoa powder a)natural (non – alkalized) and b)Dutch process (alkalized).

a. ***Dutch*** –process cocoa has been treated with a chemical, such as potassium carbonate, to reduce the natural acidity of the cocoa beans. Dutching also darkens the cocoa to an appetizing rich, deep reddish –brown color; extreme Dutching results in the distinctively flavored charcoal – black cocoa used to make Oreo cookies. Dutch –process cocoa may or may not be labeled as such, but cocoa processed with alkali should appear on the ingredient statement.

a. ***Naturalcocoa*** is typically labeled cocoa. – Generally, higher fat content improves the flavor and quality of cocoa. Natural cocoas contain 1to 12 percent fat, although superior –quality, high – fat natural cocoa is available with 22 to 24 percent fat. The flavour is fruiter and mellow.

Types of chocolate –

a. ***Semi –Sweet Chocolate*** –Made from unsweetened chocolate (chocolate liquor), but with the addition of sugar, cocoa butter, lecithin and vanilla mixed in. Semi –sweet chocolate must contain at least 35% unsweetened chocolate, and typically is less than 50%.

b. ***Dark Chocolate*** –The rules regarding classification of chocolate in this category vary throughout the world. However, the one constant is that this type of chocolate contains no milk solids, but has sweeteners and cocoa butter added to the mix. In Europe, dark chocolate must consist of at least 35% cocoa solids while in the U.S., it must have a 15% concentration of chocolate liquor.

Milk Chocolate –Like you'd guess from the name, milk chocolate is made with condensed or powdered milk. In Europe, milk chocolate must consist of at least 25% cocoa solids, while in the US, it must have10% concentration of chocolate liqueur and a minimum of 12% milk solids. Milk chocolate is primarily used for eating and is the most popular form of chocolate in the U.S.

c. ***White Chocolate*** –The name given to white chocolate is a misnomer because it isn't really chocolate at all. Strictly speaking, chocolate is defined as any product 100% based on cocoa solid. White chocolate doesn't contain any cocoa solids and is made from cocoa butter, milk solids and sugar.

<u>Couverture Chocolate</u> –Chocolates under this classification are true gourmet chocolates that are rich in cocoa butter (upwards of 35%) which creates an extremely high fat content. Cocoa butter is the fat extracted from chocolate liquor. These chocolates contain a very high percentage of cocoa which is the solid powder left after the cocoa butter is extracted from the chocolate liquor. . In family or bakers' chocolate the cocoa fat content is replaced by a vegetable –based fat. This has a detrimental effect on the texture and hardness of the chocolate but makes the product cheaper to purchase and easier to use. When used for making chocolates, decorations or moulded chocolates, couverture first has to go through a process of tempering called 'pre –crystallization'.

<u>Self –life and storage of chocolates:</u>The ideals temperature for storing chocolate is 12 – 200C, and the temperature should not fluctuate. At higher temperature the chocolate becomes soft and will lose its sheen, and

at lower temperature it may be affected by condensation. Chocolate that has been stored at a lower temperature should, when required for use, be left to acclimatize in its original packaging for a few hours until it reaches ambient temperature.

Chocolate is sensitive to humidity and easily absorbs smells and flavours. It is also liable to oxidization if it is exposed to light, direct sunlight and air for too long. Therefore, chocolate should be stored in a cool, dry place, completely sealed from light and air. Always ensure that the packaging is resealed after using.

Finished products are also very sensitive to temperature, foreign smells, flavours, light, air and humidity and to the effects of time and transportation. Typical changes that can occur during storage of chocolate products include –

- ***Fat bloom*** – a thin layer of fat crystals on the surface of the chocolate. The chocolate loses its sheen and a soft, milky white bloom appears on the surface, giving the finished chocolate an unattractive appearance. Fat bloom is caused when fats in the chocolate crystallize or when the fats in the ganache/filling migrate to the chocolate layer. The appearance of fat bloom can be delayed by storing the chocolate at a constant temperature of 10 – 150C.

- ***Sugar bloom*** – in contrast to fat bloom, sugar bloom creates a rough, coarse layer on top of the chocolate. Sugar bloom is mainly caused by condensation, which can form on the surface of chocolate if storage temperatures are too low or if the chocolate is left in a refrigerator for too long. This moisture will dissolve the sugar within the chocolate and when the moisture evaporates, the sugar re –crystallizes on the surface. Avoid rapid changes of temperature to help prevent this occurrence.

If the storage time for chocolate can be kept short, the quality of the product will be much better. Each type of chocolate will have a different shelf life, which is measured from the initial production date and is shown on the packaging. Because of the milk fat solids present in white and milk chocolate, these have shorter shelf lives than dark chocolate. Chocolates that contain a filling need special consideration. Chocolates made with cream or butter filling have a very short storage life (the recipes shown in this chapter have a shelf life of one week), provided they are stored in ideal conditions. The substitution of cream or butter with alternative ingredients (such as light sugar solutions) will help to increase shelf life.

Functions of Chocolate:

It provides structure. Baked goods are a careful balance of rough, load bearing structural ingredients (think of flour and egg white like concrete and steel beams) and tenderizers (such as sugar, fat, and egg yolks) that keep cake softer than bread. Chocolate has a lot of fat, but it winds up adding more structure than tenderness to baked goods. Cakes or cookies with cocoa powder need less flour than those without, and a sweet made with dark chocolate will be tougher than one made with milk.

It adds texture: What makes mousse, frosting, glaze, and ganache so addictive? Fat! And the more fat you add, the smoother and creamier those sweets will be. High-fat chocolate enhances those creamy textures in dairy-based chocolate sweets like mousse.

It provides flavour and colour to the product: When used alone in cakes, cocoa powder imparts a full rich chocolate flavor and dark color. Cocoa powder can also be used in recipes with other chocolates (unsweetened or dark) and this combination produces a cake with a more intense chocolate flavor than if the cocoa wasn't present. Most recipes call for sifting the cocoa powder with the flour but to bring out its full flavor it can be combined with a small amount of boiling water.

It absorbs moisture. Flour soaks up the water in eggs, butter, and milk, which you need for a solid baked good. Cocoa powder does the same, and pound for pound it can absorb more liquid than flour. So if you're adding cocoa to a cookie or cake you can decrease the flour.

CHAPTER XIII

FRUITS AND NUTS

Fruits and nuts play an important role in Bakery and confectionary products. Fruits which may be fresh ones or dried ones and different kinds of nuts increases the flavour and taste of the products and furthermore provide a definite volume of the product. They impart the essential nutrients and acids and thus increase the nutritional value of the products. Fruits and nuts should be used carefully while making any bakery or confectionary item and for that one has to know the characteristic of each of them. Fresh fruits or canned fruits contain lots of moisture and sugar and thus the recipe must be adjusted accordingly.

> "*Fruit provides a ready source of energy because it is rich in sugar (fructose), minerals and vitamin. It is also a good source of dietary fiber, both in the edible skin and in the water – soluble fiber called pectin found in certain fruits such as apples and quinces. Almost all fruit has a low calorie count.*"

Fruits: These are usually edible reproductive body having sweet pulp of a seed –bearing part of a flowering plant or tree that can be eaten as food.

Classification of fruits:

1. Berries– They are single fleshy fruits without stone, and they have a lot of seeds. Berries may be used fresh or dried.

- ***Black berries*** – belong to the *Rosaceae* family and is composed of a group of small berries or druplets. The soft fruit is popular for use in desserts, jams, and seedless jellies and sometimes wine. It is often mixed with apples for pies and crumbles.
- ***Currants*** – are small round berries obtained from shrub like plants form *Grossulariaceae*family. Currants are of two types – red and black and the pulp and juices are used in variety of bakery and confectionary products like muffins, jam and jellies. They are basically used as flavouring and colouring purposes.
- ***Rasp berries*** – Straw berries –are bright red elongated berries obtained from vine like climbers of *Rosaceae* family. It is cross between a loganberry and the black raspberry developed in Scotland. The juices and the pulps and slices of it may be used as flavouring, stuffing, decorating and spreading of muffins, cakes, pastries, pies, ice creams and toffees.
- ***Blue berries*** – are fruits from a perennial plant of *Ericaceae* family. It is native of North America and Europe. The pulp and the juices are used to make jams, jellies and fillings for cakes and pies. It can be mixed with cream and used to decorate cakes and pastries.
- ***Tay berries*** – is a cultivated shrub from *Rosaceae* family. Most cranberries are processed into products such as juice, sauce, jam and sweetened dried cranberries. It is cross between a loganberry and the black raspberry developed in Scotland. The fruit is elongated inform and is much sweeter and aromatic than loganberries. They are used similarly as raspberries and loganberries.
- ***Logan berries*** – is a hybrid of rasp berries and black berries. It is smaller in size with tan brownish red in colour. The juices and pulps are extensively used in

making pies, candies, syrups and flavouring of cakes and muffins. fruit of perennial plant grown in moist temperate regions. is a cultivated shrub from *Rosaceae* family. The fruit is elongated inform and is much sweeter and aromatic than loganberries. They are used similarly as raspberries and loganberries.They are used to prepare juices, jams and jellies and are used as garnishes for cakes and pies. The color of raspberries may extend from light pink to darker ones or they may be yellowish.

- ***Cranberries*** – are a group of evergreen dwarf shrubs or trailing vines from *Ericaceae* family grown in America and Canada. Usually cranberries as fruit are cooked into a compote or jelly, known as cranberry sauce. It is used in baking to prepare muffins, scones and cakes.

2. Citrus fruits– these are sour in nature, basically round or oval in shape containing high concentration of vitamin C.

- ***Grape fruit*** – is a subtropical citrous fruit, known for its sweet bitter taste. It looks similar to oranges, but is juicier. It is used in preparation of toffees, candies, jellies, marmalade etc.

  Lemon – These are the natives of Asia. The plant is native to south Asia and the Asia –Pacific. Culinary uses include candying and kumquat preserves, marmalade, and jelly. The juices are used in cooking and baking. These are very rich source of citric acids. Even the rind is used as flavouring agent for bakery items.
- ***Lime*** – are fruits that grow all the year round. They are smaller than lemons and are highly acidic. They are found in all over the world and are incredibly used in

making jellies, juices, marmaldes, cordials etc.

Orange – One of the distinguishing features of the satsuma is the distinctive thin, leathery skin dotted with large and prominent oil glands, which is lightly attached around the fruit, enabling it to be peeled very easily in comparison to other citrus fruits.

- ***Tangerines*** – Tangerines can be added to cakes and pies. They can also be used in breads. Tangerines are thought to have originated in China. Tangerines reached Europe in the early 19th century and came to the United States in the mid –19th century. They are smaller than oranges, with easy –to –peel skin.
- ***Satsuna*** – is a seedless and easy –peeling citrus mutant of Japanese origin introduced to the West. The fruit is sweet and usually seedless, about the size of other mandarin oranges, smaller than an orange. It is the most commonly grown in the tropical region of the world. These citrous, sweet fruit finds its use in bakery and confectionary in the preparation of jam, jellies, marmalades and juices used in confections.
- ***Clementine*** – these belong to orange family with deep orange coloured and smooth, glossy exterior appearance. They have their origination from China, but later names in Algeria after Clément Rodier. The fruit separate easily into seven to fourteen fat –juicy segments , which are very easy to peel. They are typically juicy and sweet, with less acid than oranges.
- ***Mandarin*** – The Mandarin orange, also known as the mandarin or mandarine , is a small citrus tree with fruit resembling other oranges. Mandarin oranges are usually eaten plain or in fruit salads or may used as oranges.
- ***Kumquat – or Cumquats*** are a group of small fruit –bearing shrubs in the flowering plant family *Rutaceae.*

The plant is native to south Asia and the Asia – Pacific. Culinary uses include candying and kumquat preserves, marmalade, and jelly.

3. Grapes – A grape is a non –climacteric fruit, specifically a berry that grows on the perennial and deciduous woody vines of the genus *Vitis*. Grapes can be eaten raw or they can be used for making jam, juice, jelly, vinegar, wine, grape seed extracts, raisins, molasses and grape seed oil. Grapes are also used in some kinds of confectionery. They can be used fresh or dried. Grapes are of different varieties viz –

- ***Red flame grapes*** – These grapes are bright red in colour and their juices are used in many of the culinary preparations including colouring and flavouring of creams for cakes and Gateaus.
- ***Seedless grapes*** – these varieties do not have seeds in them and are basically used in dried forms like kishmish.

4. Exotic fruits:

Figs– The fruit has ridges down its sides, resembling a star in cross section. It is a citrus fruit usually used in decoration purposes.

Persimmons –is a of perennial plant from the family *Ebenaceae*, grown abundantly in United states of America. Persimmons are generally light yellow –orange to dark red –orange in color, and depending on the species, vary in size from 1.5 to 9 cm (0.5 to 4 in) in diameter, and may be spherical, acorn –, or pumpkin –shaped. They are used for decoration and garnishing of bakery and confectionary products, making of puddings and pies.

Pickly pear – is also known as Opuntia or Nopales, is the native of North America and India, where it is called cactus. It is round oval shaped fruit with large number of spines. The skin is removed and sweet fleshy is seen, which is used for making pies, puddings, jellies and candies. It is a shrub that is grown in tropical and Mediterranean region of the world. Figs are mostly used in dried form in cake, pastry and bread mixture.

Star fruits – or Carambola is the native of South and south east Asian countries as well as of the Caribbean countries. The fruit has ridges down its sides, resembling a star in cross section. It is a citrus fruit usually used in decoration purposes.

5. Melons:

- ***Water melon*** – is grown in Asian and African countries. These fruits are grown in vine like trailer plants near the water bodies. The fruit is entirely fleshy with lots of seeds .the flesh contains almost 75% water , so juice is the main product of water melon. The seeds are also used in preparation of fondants, carvings and other decorations.
- ***Musk melon*** – belongs to the species of melon. Muskmelon is native to Persia (Iran), Armenia, and adjacent areas on the west and the east. In addition to their consumption when fresh, melons are sometimes dried.
- ***Honey dew***– they also belong to the group of musk melons with whiter smooth surface. They are the locals of North America and France. They have similar uses as of musk melons.
- ***Casaba*** – these yellow coloured tipped melon do not have much of flavour, but can be stored for a longer

time. They form attractive center pieces, so they can be used in decorating, pastries, pies and even as fillers in cakes.

6. Stone fruits:

- ***Peaches*** – are edible juicy fruits obtained from peach tree which is the native of China. It is a deciduous small tree of the family *Rosaceae.* The fruit has yellow or whitish flesh, a delicate aroma, and velvety skin. It is used for preparation of sauce, juice, jellies and many of the bakery products.
- ***Apricots*** – It is a sweet and sour fruit obtained from a small tree of the family *Rosaceae.* The fruit is a drupe similar to a small peach, 1.5–2.5 cm diameter, from yellow to orange, often tinged red; its surface can be smooth or with very short hairs. They have smother stone than other stone fruits and the skin has waxy coating. The single seed is enclosed in a hard stony shell, often called a "stone", with a grainy, smooth texture except for three ridges running down one side. It is native of Europe and Asia. Used in garnishing and decoration, pies and puddings
- ***Cherries*** – are flesh stone fruits of the family of *Prunus.* These dark red coloured round fruits grown in bunch. They are of immense use in bakery and confectionary for garnishing and decoration. They are used in preparation of certain tarts and pies.
- ***Nectarines*** – these are peach like identical fruits only exception that its skin is smooth, rather than furry. Moreover they are smaller than peaches and have spicier taste. They are the native of China. Their use is similar to that of peaches.

- ***Plum*** – these are tan reddish pink fruits obtained from small plants of the family of *Rosacea*. Damsons – The damson or damson plum is an edible drupaceous fruit, a subspecies of the plum tree. They are commonly used in the preparation of jams and jellies. They are grown in Europe. Because of its acidic, tart flavour, damsons are commercially grown for preparation in jellies, jams, pies and puddings.
- ***Greenages*** – are the fruits from France. These are plum like green coloured fruits sometimes changes into light yellow. The flesh is very juicy and sweet. They are found in tropical –temperate regions of the earth. They are used to make sauce, jam and jellies and sometimes as fillers of certain type of cakes. They are known for its rich confectionary flavor. They are considered as the finest dessert plum. They are used as sauces, juices, and find place in cakes pies and candies.
- ***Lichees*** – these are fruits from *Soapberry* family plant grown widely in Southern Asia. The fresh fruit has delicate white flesh with a big smooth round stone in it. They are used in preparation of jams, jellies, syrup and juices.

7. Tropical fruits:

- ***Bananas*** – Bananas – are common plant from the family of *Musaceae*. They may be yellow, purple or red in colour and mostly found in south Asian countries. Due to its sweety and mushy nature, they find their use in variety of ways in the house. They are used as fillers, as decorating agents' binders, find place in pies, puddings, cakes etc.

- ***Kiwis*** –The kiwifruit, often shortened to kiwi in many parts of the world, is the edible berry from the family of *Actinidiaceae*, about the size of a large hen's egg (5–8 cm / 2–3 in long and 4.5–5.5 cm / 1¾–2 in diameter). It has a fibrous, dull brown –green skin and bright green or golden flesh with rows of tiny, black, edible seeds. The fruit has a soft texture and a sweet but unique flavour, and today is a commercial crop in several countries, mainly in Italy, New Zealand, Brazil and Chile. This fruit has original native of America, but nowadays grown all over the world. The tree like plant from the family *Caricaceae,* bears oval shaped fruits like avocado, but bears large number of black coloured seeds when ripe. Dates – is an edible sweet fruit obtained from date palm (family Arecaceae), has its origination in and around Persian gulf. Dates are oval –cylindrical, 3–7 cm long, and 2–3 cm diameter. They are used in dried form in the preparation of breads, pies and candies.
- ***Mangoes*** – The mango is a fleshy stone fruit from the family Anacardiaceae. They are grown in in the Indian sub –continent. Mangoes are used in the preparation of juices, pulp,puddings, pastries and cakes .they are also used in preparation of candies and toffees.
- ***Papayas***– It is primarily used in decoration, but can also be used in preparation of muffins, cakes and gateaus.It is used in preparation of jellies, pulp, pies and puddings.
- ***Pineapples*** – are common tropical fruits from the family of *Bromeliaceae.* This herbaceous and perennial plant is made of a number of coalesced berries. Pineapples are used as fresh or tinned in a number of bakery and confectionary products like cakes, gateaus, pastries, candies, and toffees. Sometimes they are also used in garnishing and decoration of baked products.

Cooking of fruits for bakery and confectionary:

The use of fruits in cooking dated back hundreds of years. While fruits are most commonly used in desserts in foods such as cookies, muffins, yoghurt, ice cream and cakes. Not only are fruits used in preparing a variety of dishes, but they also help keep certain foods fresh and help preserve their colour. There are various ways to cook fruit, and certain consideration should be made beforehand as fruit tends to delicate, and can disintegrate easily.

Generally, boiling is too harsh a method for most fruits; gentle simmering preserves the texture and shape of fruits. When cooking soft and stone fruits, simply warm them by placing them in a pan of boiled water and then used accordingly. Poaching fruit is a similar method, and is a common way to cook fruits such as pears. Bring the water to a simmer and then gently lower the fruit into the pan with a spoon. Immediately reduce the heat so the liquid is barely bubbling, and cook until the fruit is tender. You could also stew fruit, where the saucepan is covered and the fruit is cooked in just enough liquid to cover it. This method helps keep it moist. Fruit poaches well in most liquids, from plain water to dense sugar syrup to wine poached pears in red wine with ginger sauce.

It is important to make sure that while stewing a fruit, the water ratio is not too high or else all the nutrients will get expelled in the water and the fruit will be left only with fibrous part. Use just enough moisture to cook the fruit. Fruit such as apples and pears can be grilled or stewed to make them soft and palatable so that they can be incorporated in the recipe. This is because they are able to hold their shape and texture while cooking. Softer fruits such as peaches, nectarines, plums and mangoes may become soft if overcooked. Peeled fruits should not be stored in open, as the enzymes and minerals come in contact with the air and oxidize, becoming brown to dark tan in colour. So, once the fruits are peeled and cut, they should be soaked in water, or sugar syrup. Adding 1tsp of lemon juice to the water will help the fruit preserve its colour. Some fruits like oranges, apples, bananas, grapefruits may be pureed and stored for future use. Fruit jams, jellies and marmalades are widely used in kitchens.

Dried fruits like apples, guavas, cherries, plums, dates, prunes, apricot, figs, bananas etc are also widely used in bakery and confectionary. As they are dry, so they can be used as it is, or may be soaked in sugar syrup and then used.

Drying is also a good way for preserving fruits and it intensifies their flavours. Most fruits can be dried effectively.

Dried fruits:

A fruit dried to loose most of its moisture, accumulates natural sugars, and keeps almost indefinitely is called as dried fruit. This has been practiced in the Middle Eastern people for over 5000 years. They have preserved dates, figs and apricots by sun drying.

Commonly used dried fruits –

- **Apples** – Apples attract moisture and so have shorter shelf life than other dried fruit. They can be eaten alone or used in baking or as toppings for breakfast cereals

- **Apricots and Peaches** – They can be eaten on their own and are used with meats.
- **Currants, sultanas and raisins** – Currant is a tiny berry related to the gooseberry. There are black, red and white currants. A raisin is simply a dried grape. Grapes are either sun –dried or dehydrated mechanically. Sultanas are large, succulent and often –seedless grapes.
- **Prunes**– These are whole dried plums. They can be canned or preserved in brandy or vinegar. They are sold pitted and un –pitted. Prunes are very popular as a stewed breakfast fruit.
- **Bananas** – Drying concentrates the elusive taste of the banana to produce delicious chewy texture.
- **Figs**– are generally used dry. They are chopped or sliced for use in cakes, pies etc.

<u>Uses of fruits –</u>

- Dried fruit is sweeter and richer than fresh fruit, which makes it invaluable in baking and desserts.
- It is most often used in fruitcakes, puddings and mousse and occasionally in making various stuffing.
- It can be eaten on its own, candied or used as a confectionery item.
- Fruits can be pureed to make jam, jelly and marmalades used as fillings, toppings and piping of cakes and biscuits.
- They can also be used as toppings for cereals, creams, yoghurt and custards.

<u>Nuts:</u>

Nuts are single seeded dry hard –shelled fruits that have to be cracked to open.Nuts can also be described as any seed or fruit with an edible kernel in a hard or brittle shell.

Varieties of nuts –

- **Almonds** – They have a crunchy texture and a rich, delicate flavour that's especially good in desserts, like candy, ice cream, tortes, and coffee cake. Almonds can be bought shelled or unshelled, blanched, sliced, slivered, ground, or chopped.
- **Pistachios** – These Middle Eastern nuts are crunchy and delicately sweet and can be used in almost everything, from ice cream to pilaffs. They are encased in shells, which are sometimes dyed red.
- **Pecans**– This nut is a popular baking ingredient in the South America, and for good reason! Pecans develop a rich flavor, and brittle, crunchy texture when baked. Use pecan halves in pies and cookies, or grind them up with butter and sugar to create decadent gluten –free pie crust!
- **Cashew Nuts** – These rich, sweet nuts have a toxic shell, so they're almost always sold shelled. Used in dessert, toppings, for garnish etc.,
- **Chestnut** – These sweet, starchy, low –fat nuts are quite common in southern Europe. Chestnuts are used as stuffing for turkeys. Chestnut puree is used in pastries and gateaux.
- **Peanut** – These are not nuts, but legumes that grow underground. They are cheaper than most nuts, and are often eaten by hand. They are incorporated into candies, stir –fries, or used in pastes to make certain gravies in Indian cuisine and in making pie fillings.

- **Coconut** – The coconut is a very useful and versatile food ingredient. The flesh used to make many pastes and fish curries especially, the water used to make drinks and coconut milk is used to finish many soups and curries. The desiccated dry variety is also used in cakes and confectionery.
- **Walnuts**– have a mild, buttery flavor that makes them perfect for baking into cookies and cakes. They have high oil content, so they tend to toast much faster than other varieties. Because of this, it's best to use raw walnuts to prevent them from burning during the baking process.
- **Brazil nut**– As the name suggests, this nut is native to brazil and an attempt to cultivate this in any other country has failed. The Brazil nut tree is around 150 ft tall and 6 ft in diameter. The size of the fruit of this tree is 3kg and contains 15 –20 seeds from which the nuts are obtained.
- **Beech nut**– These are native to temperate Europe, Asia and North America. The fruit is a small, sharply three–angled nut 10–15 mm long, borne singly or in pairs in soft –spine husks 1.5–2.5 cm long, known as cupules. The nuts are edible, though bitter (though not nearly as bitter as acorns) with high tannin content, and are called *beechnuts* or *beechmast*.
- **Macadamias** – It is the nut of a small evergreen tree, and is very common in Australia and Hawaii. It is similar to hazelnut in looks; the only difference is that it is probably 3 times bigger than a hazelnut. This nut is most commonly used with light, tropical flavors like pineapple or white chocolate. They are high in oil, so they take on a deep buttery flavor and texture when baked.

- **Charoli** –are tiny almond –flavoured dried seeds of a bush called *Buchananialanzan*, which is cultivated across India, primarily in the northwestern India. After the hard shell is cracked, the stubby seed within is as soft as a pine nut.
- **Pine nut** – Pine nuts are the edible seeds of pines, which are grown at higher altitudes of Asia and America. They are used as toppings and pastes for cakes and pies.
- **Candle nut** – Candlenut trees are native to the tropical northern rainforests of Australia, the Moluccas Islands, Malaysia, and are found on many islands in the South Pacific. Candle nuts are cream –colored, soft, oily seeds within a hard – shelled nut with flavour of macadamia nut. Roasted slivers or shavings of candle nut have a pleasing, nutty, almond –like flavor without the background bitterness characteristic of almonds.
- **Hazel nut** – The hazelnut looks like as chickpea and is a enclosed in a brown shell. It often resembles as heart shape and is mostly grown in Europe and China. These are used in making nut butters and marzipan, in cakes and ice creams. It also adds flavor to all baked goods.
- **Kola nut** – The kola is a star –shaped fruit of the kola tree, indigenous to West Africa. Each fruit contains between two and five kola nuts. About the size of a chestnut, this little fruit is packed with caffeine. Kola nuts have a bitter taste when chewed fresh. When they're dried, the taste becomes milder and they reportedly smell of nutmeg and are used with chocolate.

Handling nuts:

Nuts can be used in variety of ways as seen table15.3. Generally nuts can be processed in the following ways.

- Nuts can easily chop if they are warm and moist as most of the nuts contain oil and hence they become more pliable if warmed.
- Roasting or toasting nuts brings out their flavor and once shelled and skinned they can be placed in a medium oven (175^{0}C).
- Nuts can be blanched in hot water for a couple of minutes to remove the skin. This is usually done for pistachio nuts as blanching deepens the colour and also for almonds to make it into a paste for making marzipans etc.

Selection and storage of nuts: Unshelled nuts keep well almost anywhere if they are protected from heat, air, light and moisture. Shelled nuts on the other hand, do not keep as well, and should be stored tightly covered in a cool dark and dry place. Fresh nuts available are with their shell and are best for long storage. Nuts in their shell should be heavy for their size, and intact with no cracks or holes. The larger the size of the nut, the better will be the taste. Unshelled nuts are sold in bulk and may be roasted or raw, left whole, slivered, sliced or broken into large pieces. Any nut with visible mould should be avoided. All these forms have specific used in the kitchen.

Certain factors to be kept in mind while storing nuts are given below:

- As nuts contain substantial amounts of oil and easily turn rancid, exposure to light, moisture, or heat will reduce their shelf life.

- Nuts are best kept in their original packaging, airtight containers, refrigerators or freezers if kept longer than a month.
- For short periods nuts can be stored in an air tight container in a dark cool place.
- Nuts in their shells keep longer than any form of processed nuts. Freezing nuts with their shell in is best.
- Nuts that are soft or stale may be partially restored by roasting in the oven.
- Salted nuts have a freezer storage life if six months as compared to plain ones, which can keep up to 12 months.
- Toasting and roasting reduce the freezer storage life, so delay toasting and roasting rill required.
- Nuts and seed should be used directly from the freezer without thawing.

Packaged nuts may be processed with preservatives and dyes, and are often heavily seasoned with salt. Dry roasted nuts usually so not have any additional fat but may be roasted with different types of fat. To ensure storage, nuts dipped in chocolate, spiced nuts, sugared or yogurt coated nuts are also available.

CHAPTER XIV

BAKERY EQUIPMENTS AND TOOLS

Having the proper tools and equipment for a Particular task may mean the difference between a job well done and one done carelessly, incorrectly or even dangerously. Listing of various essential pieces of bakery equipment for small or hotel kitchen is the most important task to do during bakery setup. Without proper bakery equipment and tools the bakery will not be able to produce good product. Hence knowledge of bakery equipment is very important during any kind of bakery set up.

Bakery equipments and tools can be classified into 8 categories, they are –

1. OVENS:

- ***Convection oven*** – A convection oven (also known as a fan –assisted oven or simply a fan oven) is an oven that has fans to circulate hot air around food,reducing hot and cool spots and helping dishes on every rack cook more evenly.

    - ***Rotary oven*** – Designed with a turntable, industrial electric rotary ovens move materials in circular motions inside the heat chamber. As the process picks up pace, the hearth can be rotated on a continuous basis, manually and with the help of an indicator.

- ***Deck or cabinet oven*** – Deck ovens are so called because the items to be baked— either on sheet pans or, in the case of some breads, freestanding—are placed directly on the bottom, or deck, of the oven. There are no racks for holding pans in deck ovens. Deck ovens are also called stack ovens because several bread doughs may be stacked on top of one another.
- ***Rack Oven*** – A rack oven is a large oven into which entire racks full of sheet pans can be wheeled for baking. Normal baker's racks hold 8 to 24 full –size sheet pans, but racks made specifically to go into rack ovens usually hold 15 to 20 pans. Rack ovens hold 1 to 4 of these racks at once. The ovens are also equipped with steam injectors.
- ***Microwave oven*** – Microwave ovens are electrically powered ovens used to cook or reheat foods. They are available in a range of sizes and power settings. Microwave ovens do not brown foods unless fitted with special browning elements, however. In the bakeshop, microwave ovens are useful as a convenience device for melting chocolate or butter.

2. OTHER BAKING EQUIPMENTS:

- ***Double boiler*** – A double boiler is a set of two pans nested together, with enough room in the bottom pan for 1 or 2 inches of water. Double boilers are used to cook or heat foods that need gentle heat, such as melting chocolate. The water in the bottom pan is brought to a simmer, and the second pan is set on top.

- ***Proving chamber or Proofer*** – is a special box in which the ideal conditions for fermenting yeast doughs can be created. The box maintains a preset warm temperature and humidity level appropriate to the specific dough.
- ***Dough sheeter*** – The dough sheeter is an electric appliance that mechanically rolls dough and pastry to a uniform thickness. The device consists of a cloth conveyor belt that moves beneath a stationary rolling pin. The height of the pin is adjusted to change the thickness of the product.

3. PREPARATORY EQUIPMENTS:

- ***Strainers and Sieves*** – Strainers and sieves are used primarily to aerate and remove impurities from dry ingredients and drain or purée cooked foods. Strainers, colanders, drum sieves and china caps (chinois) are non –mechanical devices with a stainless steel mesh or screen through which food passes. The size of the mesh or screen varies from extremely fine to several millimeters wide; select the fineness best suited for the task at hand.
- ***Icing comb*** – A small plastic tool, usually triangular, with serrated edges in various patterns, for decorating icings and other pastry and decorative items.
- ***Pastry brush*** – Soft bristle bakery equipment or a brush, useful for coating the tops of pastries and pie crusts with an egg wash or milk, or for greasing baking pans with melted butter or shortening. Once upon a time, brushes were made of animal hair, but these days, a better option is one with silicone bristles, which don't fall out and are

heat – and bacteria – resistant as well.

- ***Pastry blender*** – This is a cooking utensil used to mix a hard (solid) fat into flour in order to make pastries.The tool is usually made of narrow metal strips or a wire attached to a handle, and is used by pressing down on the items to be mixed (known as "cutting in"). It is also used to break these fats (shortening, butter, lard) into smaller pieces.
- ***Spoons and ladle*** – Long –handled ladles are useful for portioning liquids such as sauces, custards and syrups. The capacity, in ounces or milliliters, is stamped on the handle.
- ***Portion scoops*** – (also known as dishers) resemble ice cream scoops. They come in a range of standardized sizes and have a lever –operated blade for releasing their contents. Scoops are useful for portioning muffin batters and cookie dough or other soft foods.
- ***Rubber spatula*** – A broad flexible rubber or plastic tip on a long handle, used to scrape bowls and pans and also in folding of egg foams or whipped cream.
- ***Rolling pins*** – These are cylindrical food preparation utensil used to shape and flatten dough. Two styles of rolling pin are found– rollers and rods. Roller types consists of a thick cylinder are mounted on ball bearings with handles at either end. Rod type rolling pins are usually thin tapered batons.
- ***Pastry cloth*** – Usually made of durable cotton canvas, a pastry cloth makes an excellent work surface for rolling out pie crusts, biscuits, cookies, and other doughs. Rubbing a little flour into the cloth prevents sticking without adding excess flour to the dough, keeping the pastry light and flaky.

- ***Hand gloves*** – An oven glove, or oven mitt, is an insulated glove or mitten usually worn in the kitchen to easily protect the wearer's hand from hot objects such as ovens, stoves, cookware, etc.
- ***Rotating cake stand*** – A rotating cake stand is a structuralstool in which a round, flat disk that swivels freely on a pedestal base.It is used for decorating cakes and pastries. Cake stands are a form of tableware; they come in different materials like wood, pottery, metal, etc.
- ***Pastry bag and nozzles***– Cone shape cloth or plastic bag with open end that can be fitted with nozzles of various shapes and sizes. Used to pipe icing on cakes, desserts, dough etc.
- ***Offset Spatula*** – Offset spatulas, sometimes called cake spatulas or decorating spatulas, feature a narrow metal blade with a wooden handle. The metal has a pair of bends in it so that the blade sits about half an inch lower than the handle. This makes it easier to frost the center of a cake without your knuckles bumping into the edges.

4. MEASURING TOOLS:

While many aspects of bread baking are creative and artistic, baking is first and foremost a science. Accurately measuring the ingredients is a critical part of artisan bread baking.

- ***Volume measurers*** – Ingredients may be measured by volume using measuring spoons and measuring cups, though most professional bakeshops use scales to measure all but the smallest quantities. Measuring spoons sold as a set usually include ¼ tsp, ½ tsp, 1tsp and 1 tbsp units.Liquid measuring cups are available in capacities from 1 cup to 1 gallon. They are also sold in sets of ¼ cup, 1/3 –cup, ½ cup and 1 cup units.

- ***Weighing machine*** – The balance scale works by comparing the ingredient to be weighed against a known mass. The ingredient to be weighed is placed on one side of the scale, and weights are either placed on the opposite side or moved along a beam until the two sides are in balance.Compression scales use a platform mounted on a spring to measure weight– As the platform is compressed from the weight of the ingredient, the spring compresses proportionally to the force being applied to it. They are available calibrated in gms, ounces or pounds. Digital scales, the preferred equipment for these formulas, are easy to use and very accurate in the kitchen. Inside the scale is a small computer that calculates the weight based on the resistance measured on the strain gauge, a small electrical component.

- ***Thermometer*** – Various types of thermometers and gauges are used in the bakeshop to determine when foods are fully cooked and when working with yeast dough, chocolate, sugar and other ingredients. Stem –type or probe thermometers, including instant –read models, are inserted into foods to obtain temperature readings. Temperatures are shown on either a dial noted by an arrow or a digital readout. An instant –read thermometer is a small stem –type model, designed to be carried in a pocket and used to provide quick temperature readings.

- ***Timer*** – Portable kitchen timers are useful for any busy chef. Small digital timers can be carried in a pocket; some even time three functions at once. Select a timer with a loud alarm signal and long timing capability.

5. MIXING TOOLS:

- ***Mixing bowls*** – These are a deep bowl of different sizes that is particularly well suited for mix in ingredients together in.
- ***Wooden spoon*** – Wooden spoons are strong and durable, withstand heat, won't scratch nonstick pans, and perfect for stirring almost anything, including hot liquids like sugar on the stovetop.
- ***Bench scrapper/dough scrapper*** – A broad stiff piece of metal with a wooden handle on one edge, used to cut pieces of dough and to scrape workbenches. It is used for working with sticky bread doughs, dividing and lifting portions, and scraping extra bits off your work surface. Dough scrapers are also handy for pulling up delicate pastry dough and transferring it to a pie pan without breaking.
- ***Planetary mixer*** – this vertical mixer is the most common type used in baking, used in mixing dough and preparation of batters. It has three attachments – The paddle is a flat blade used for general mixing. The wire whip is used for such tasks as beating egg foams and cream. The dough arm or hook is used for mixing and kneading yeast doughs. Dough hooks may be standard J –hooks or spiral hooks.

- ***Hand blender*** – is a simple –to –use kitchen gadget that is used for blending eggs, creaming, pureeing soups, making single drinks, or blending milkshakes in small quantities.
- ***Whisker*** – Loops of stainless steel wire fasten to a handle. Heavy whisks are straight/stiff and have relatively few wires. Used for general mixing and beating of heavy liquids. Balloon whisks or piano wire whisks have many flexible wires used to whip eggs, cream, hollandaise and mixing thinner liquids.

6. CUTTING TOOLS:

- ***Kitchen knives*** – various types and sizes like plain, one side serrated, both side serrated.
- ***Pastry wheel/cutter*** – A round rotating blade on a handle used for cutting rolled out doughs and pastry or baked pizza.
- ***Biscuit and doughnut cutter*** – various cutters of different shapes and sizes are used to cut cookie and biscuit doughs and doughnut.
- ***Chopping boards*** – boards made of acrylic fibre are used as cutting base.
- ***Graters*** – Four sided metal box with different sized grids, used to shred vegetables, cheese, citrus rinds and other foods.
- ***Zester*** – Small hand bakery equipment to remove the zest of citrus fruits in thin strips.

7. BAKING PANS:

- ***Bundt pan or Tube center pan*** – Pan with a hollow tube in the center.The tube is used to conduct heat through the center of a cake, ensuring that the cake bakes evenly.
- ***Bread moulds/Loaf pan*** – these are rectangular or square metallic pan moulds with or without lid, used in baking brads and loaf. They are available in different shapes and sizes. The most useful sizes are a 9¼ x 5¼ x 2 ½ inch loaf pans for larger loaves and 8 ½ x 4 ½ x 2 ½ inch loaf pans for smaller loaves
- ***Muffin pan*** – are a rectangular metal baking pan with six or twelve cup, used to bake both muffins and cupcakes.A standard muffin pan has 12 cups, each measuring about 2¾ inches at the top and 1 –3/8 inches deep. Mini muffin pans normally have either 12 or 24 cups and measure about 1¾ inch across the top and ¾ inch deep
- ***Baking cups*** – Baking cups are paper or foil cups used to line muffin or cupcake pans. Muffin pan sizes are typically mini, standard, and jumbo sized.
- ***Popover Pans***– Popover pans have deep, narrow cups, which force the popover batter to rise up and out, producing the typical tall popover shape.
- ***Cake pans*** – Many basic cake recipes use traditional round layer cake pans that are either 8 or 9 inches in diameter. The pans should be at least 2 or 2 ½ inches deep so that the batter doesn't overflow.
- ***Jelly roll pan*** – These are the same as a baking sheet. They have a raised edge allaround, usually ½ to 1 inchhigh.

- ***Brioche Molds*** – A brioche mold is a deep, beautifully fluted round mold, made of tinned steel. They are specifically made for baking the traditional French knot – shaped brioche loaf. A small brioche mold can also be used for baking small cakes, muffins, and individual sweet breads.
- ***Flan Rings*** – A flan ring is a metal ring with no fluting around the sides, and no bottom. The ring is set on a baking sheet that is lined with parchment paper or a non –stick baking mat, and then filled. The baking sheet serves as the bottom of the pan.
- ***Baking trays*** – These are very important bakery equipment mostly aluminum or non –stick and about 2" deep. They come in a variety of shapes and sizes.
- ***Tart Pans*** – Tart pans normally have a fluted edge and 1 inch deep and may come in round, square, or rectangular shapes. They often have a removable bottom which makes is easy to remove the tart without damaging the delicate crust.
- ***Baba Molds*** – Baba molds are tall straight –sided, cylindrical shaped molds about 1 ½ to 3 inches in diameter, and 1 ½ to 4 inches in height. They are specifically designed for the classic yeast –raised sweet cakes called Babas.
- ***Custard cup*** – These are 6 ounce cups for baking custards. Their small size are also good for holding cooked puddings or other desserts, and are also useful for holding pre –measured ingredients when prepping ingredients for cookies or cakes.
- ***Baking sheets*** – have raised edges all around, and are normally the choice for professional bakers. They are a good, all –purpose pan and can be used for everything from baking cookies to toasting nuts.

- ***Cookie sheets*** – These are rimless, flat metal sheets, perfectly designed for placing rows of cookies. They normally have a small rim on the short sides for easy gripping. The long flat edges allow you to slide cookies off the sheet after baking.
- ***Pie moulds*** – different shapes and sizes are used.

8. COOLING EQUIPMENTS:

- ***Cooling rack*** –This are racks with wire mesh on which hot fresh bakery products are kept, so that vapours escape from the below also and the product gets cooled.
- ***Refrigerators*** – these cooling equipments are of three types – domestic refrigerators – the common one that can be seen in every household. Walk –in – large, room –sized box where you can walk in and is capable of holding hundreds of pounds of food on adjustable shelves. Reach –ins may be individual units or show case with several shelves and covered by glass from one side for view.

CHAPTER XV

PRODUCTION CONSIDERATIONS

The baking industry can be divided into four segments– retail, in store, restaurant/food service and wholesale. The largest volume of business is conducted by wholesale bakeries, but still many bakers have their own preferences. Entrepreneurs may choose to open their own bake shops, whereas bakers more comfortable to opt for a career in wholesale or in – store facilities.

Retail bakeries have relatively low –volume of businesses that produce and sell items directly to consumers. A retail bakery may make a wide variety of breads, cakes, cookies, pastries and desserts, or it may specialize in one or two items, such as cupcakes, bagels, wedding cakes or doughnuts.

In –store bakeries found in groceries and club stores offer a range of locally popular breads, cakes, cookies and pies. Some may be made entirely from scratch; others may be assembled from pre –made icings, frozen cakes or simple mixes.

Restaurant bakeshops produce items for the restaurant's dessert menu and for use in other areas. For example, a hotel bakeshop will produce individual plated desserts for each restaurant at the property, but may also make puff pastry and pâté dough for use in the garde manger, chocolates for room service and grand display pieces for elegant buffets.

Upscale restaurants may prepare all dessert and bread items in –house, whereas a less ambitious restaurant with a small staff may purchase its items directly from a wholesale bakery.

Wholesale bakeries produce foods that reach the final consumer through grocery stores, restaurants and hotels, or the wholesaler's own retail outlets. A large wholesale bakery may have sophisticated production equipment capable of producing hundreds, even thousands of items hourly. It may produce a range of breads, desserts, cookies and crackers, or it may specialize in one type of product, such as doughnuts.

Being a baker is a lot more than just knowing how to bake bread. Bakery and confectionery as a career is both an art and science. A baker makes various kinds of loaves, bread rolls, croissants, buns, pastries, cakes and savories by adding his own innovation to his basic knowledge of baking. In large establishment the bakery and confectionary is managed by a brigade of chefs who according to Sir Augustus Escoffier is as follows –

1. ***Executive Pastry Chef or Master baker*** – who is responsible for the entire Operation of all the kitchen.
2. ***Pastry Sous chef*** – he works as assistant to the Executive chef.
3. ***Station Chef or Chef de partie*** – he controls individual section of the bakery and confectionary.
4. ***Bread baker*** – responsible for baking different types of breads, sponges, rolls and baked dough containers used for other menu items (for example, bouchées and feuilletés).
5. ***Confectioner*** – who makes candies and petit fours.
6. ***Ice cream maker (Fr. glacier)***, who makes all chilled and frozen desserts;
7. ***Decorator (Fr. décorateur)***, who makes showpieces and special cakes.

8. ***Apprentices and helper*** – to assist the above.

Attributes of a baker –

- ***Passion*** – A good baker needs to have a high degree of passion to bring out the best for providing the utmost delight to the customers. The baker should be fond of making quality food that can bring pride to the bakery.

- ***Knowledge*** – Pastry chefs and bakers must be able to identify, purchase, use and prepare a wide variety of foods. They should be able to train and supervise a safe, skilled and efficient staff. To do all this successfully, professional pastry chefs and bakers must possess detailed knowledge of the products and understand and apply certain scientific and business principles.

- ***Excellent numerical skills*** – A good baker need to measure the ingredients and also order and plan the cooking times perfectly to bring out the best products with the best recipe.

- ***Excellent creativity*** – To stand out in the competition, a baker should have excellent creative ability and should be able something unique that can differentiate from the competitors.Creativity in baking can also be expressed through cake decoration, which can involve anything from brainstorming physics –defying cake structures to crafting elaborate sugar fondant flowers. Many cake decorators are also handy with a paintbrush and use edible paints to create wonderful details.

- ***Attention to detail*** – As we mentioned, baking is a science that relies on precise measurements and temperature conditions. All ingredients must be weighed and measured accurately. A few extra gms or an oven that's 25 degrees hotter than the recipe dictates and the baking will suffer. The best bakers in the world have a keen eye for detail while creating consistent pastry art.

- ***Patience*** – Many of us are guilty of wanting to skip to the next step when undertaking the more tedious elements of a baking recipe. It takes patience to ensure that things are done to a high standard in baking, the most common examples being whisking, creaming and mixing.

- ***The baker should be able to work under pressure*** – Providing quality baked food to the customers at the right time calls for excellent time management. It is important to understand and maintain the right time to produce the right result at the right time that can relive the stress.

- ***Good organizational skills*** – It is essential to maintain the kitchen area in perfect shape and to keep the ingredients in order. It requires a great organization skill to maintain the inventory rightly and to manage the show correctly.
- ***Awareness of safety and hygiene rules*** – Not only should your baking creations taste good; they should also reach strict hygiene standards. You want the people who consume your food to stay safe too. Some countries (especially Singapore) have stringent rules on food safety and hygiene that you should be aware of.

- ***Tidiness*** – Bakers should always strive to keep their workstation clean and organized. It is not only good in terms of food preparation, but it is important in terms of general kitchen management as customers want to be confident that the food they are eating is safe to eat and was prepared in a clean and sanitary environment.

- ***Reasonable level of physical fitness*** – As per every job, you need to be physically fit to carry out the job tasks. Baking also consists of carrying heavy trays laden with baking goods and sacks of flour and sugar etc. All these carrying require a fit body to carry out.

- ***The ability to work in a team*** – Teamwork is extremely important in a kitchen. You need to be able to work with other people to make beautiful creations on a large –scale. Communication with your team members ensures that things are done efficiently and quickly as well.

- ***Professional Pride*** – Professionals take pride in their work, and want to make sure it is something they can be proud of. A professional cook maintains a positive attitude, works efficiently, neatly, and safely, and always aims for high quality. A professional who takes pride in his or her work recognizes the talent of others in the field and is inspired and stimulated by their achievements.

Hygiene and sanitation:

- Each establishment should ensure that they follow the standard norms of Hygiene and sanitation to the utmost level.

- Only healthy workers are to be allowed to carry on production work.
- Uniforms should be always clean and tidy and proper.
- Avoid cross contamination techniques.
- Wash hands frequently.
- Dis –infect every work area , tools and equipments before the start of work.
- The work area should be properly lightened and ventilated.
- Follow safe food handling process.
- To prevent bacterial growth – keep hot food hot and cold food cold.
- Ensure efficient pest control techniques.
- Ensure proper packing and storing techniques.
- Ensure Safety to the workers.

CHAPTER XVI

STALING AND SPOILAGE

Bread is a perishable commodity, which is at its best when consumed 'fresh'. Unfortunately, bread remains 'fresh' for only a few hours after it leaves the oven. During storage it is subjected to a number of changes which lead to the loss of its natural freshness. The factors that govern the rate of freshness loss in bread during storage are mainly divided into two groups; those attributed to microbial attack, and those that are result of a series of slow chemical or physical changes which lead to the progressive firming up of the crumb, commonly referred to as 'staling'.

Bread staling is a complicated process that involves loss of aroma, changes in mouth feel, loss of crumb softness and development of crumbliness, toughening of the crust, firming of the crumb, loss of moisture and flavor and loss in product freshness. It is a term which indicates decreasing consumer acceptance of bakery products caused by changes in crumb other than those resulting from spoilage organisms.

Some of the changes which occur in bread as a result of staling are –

- Increase of crumb firmness
- Increase in crumbliness of the crumb
- Deterioration in flavour and aroma
- Loss of crust crispiness

ANTI –STALING INGREDIENTS:

1. ***Emulsifiers.*** For the past several years bakers used emulsifiers called bread softeners to produce bread that will remain soft for a longer period of time. It is added to the dough during mixing. Some of the more common ones are monoglycrides, calcium steroyllactylate, and sodium steroyllactylate. The softening action takes place after the bread is baked. Also, Potato bread will resist staling because potatoes act as anti –staling ingredients to some degree. Some anti –staling ingredients also perform as dough conditioners or dough strengtheners.
2. ***Enzymes.*** Enzyme manufacturers are hard at work on generic engineering and protein engineering producing enzymes to extend the shelf life of bread many fold. In a paper presented at the 1999 American Society of Baking's Annual Convention, it was stated that some of these enzymes are available now. However, since every baker wants to have one better, enzyme manufacturers will continue to work on developing better ones. It was also stated that there is a lag time of between 2 and 3 years between the time a specific enzyme is identified and actually having it available for the baker to use.Advantages of Using Enzymes instead of Chemicals. Since enzymes are produced from natural ingredients, they will find greater acceptance by the housewife than when chemicals are used.
3. ***Mold and Mold Inhibitors.*** Sanitation plays a very important role in preventing mold in bread. Mold spores do not survive baking temperatures. The interior of the loaf, when it comes out of the oven is about 210 to 212 degrees F. which will destroy any mold spores which

may be present in the dough. Therefore, bread and other bakery products can only be contaminated after they leave the oven.

Microbiological spoilage:

Although the ideal temperature of bread for delaying the process of staling is 110^{0}F, there are chances of microbial growth as they may find adaptable moisture and temperature. The most common microbial spoilage occurs by two agents– Moulds and bacteria and the least common of all types of microbial spoilage in bread are that caused by certain types of yeast.

Mould spoilage:

Mould spoilage of bread is due to post –processing contamination. Bread loaves fresh out of the oven are free of moulds or mould spores due to their thermal inactivation during the baking process. Bread becomes contaminated after baking from the mould spores present in the atmosphere surrounding loaves during cooling, slicing, packaging and storage. They usually form. Mould infestation can be identified by bluish green/ green or pinky coloured velvety spots on bread producing musty odour.

Prevention of mould infestation :

To prevent formation of moulds in breads, it is extremely important to follow strict hygiene and sanitation in the bakery, like –

- Proper ventilation and circulation of air.
- Area should be absolutely dry and moisture free.
- Area should be well illuminated.
- Handling bread hygienically.

- Keep on stock rotation every 24 hours. Overstocking may lead to spoilage.
- Maintaining proper room temperature.
- Follow HACCP plan.

Bacterial Spoilage:

Rope is a germ disease caused by bacteria (*bacillus mesentericus or bacillus pulmilus*). The germs are most likely to develop during hot weather in bread that is not sufficiently fermented or not well baked. This disease breaks down the cells of the bread and leaves a sticky, pasty mass. When the crumb is pressed together, and pulled apart, it will stretch into long, sticky, web –like strands. The product will have the odor of over –ripe cantaloupe, very repelling. The bacteria may be present in the ingredients, especially flour and yeast. Unlike mold, rope spores are not destroyed by baking temperatures.

Symptom of roppines –

- Repelling odour, something like over –ripe cantaloupe.
- Soury and bitterly taste
- Sticky and web –like crumb
- Reddish brown coloured crust.

Prevention of Rope disease –

- Regulate the acidity of the bread –add vinegar or acetic acid or reduce the pH
- Proper ventilation and circulation of air.
- Area should be absolutely dry and moisture free.
- Area should be well illuminated.
- Handling bread hygienically.

- Keep on stock rotation every 24 hours. Overstocking may lead to spoilage.
- Maintaining proper room temperature.
- Follow HACCP plan.

CHAPTER XVII

SCOPE OF BAKERY

Bakery industry in India today has an important place in the industrial map of the country. Bakery products are an item of mass consumption in view of its low price and high nutrient value. With rapid growth and changing eating habits of people, bakery products have gained popularity among masses. The sector, typically, constitutes cakes, breads and biscuits.

Bakery industry in India is on a growth curve. The sector which is difficult to define has indicated promising growth prospects and has been making rapid progress. The bakery industry has achieved third position in generating revenue among the processed food sector. The first and second segments are the wheat flour processing and fruits and vegetables processing, stated experts from the food industry.

The bakery industry also is a lucrative sector for entrepreneurship in the food industry. This calls for honing skills in baking science and technology. With Globalization and India being viewed as a potential growth market, there has been a profusion of bakery chains springing up across the country. These include Au Bon Pain, the US-based bakery cafe chain, Monginis, Donut Baker, Cookie Man, Croissant, Cafe Coffee Day, Oven pick, Bread Talk, SAJ Industries Bisk Farm, Hot Bread, Birdy's, Donut Master and Cookie Jar.

> "*For a bakery and cafe chains there are several challenges to meet when it comes to growth of the*

business and generating revenue. Some of the issues are procuring highest quality of ingredients, maintaining consistency in standards of food and managing efficient service in terms of hospitality."

Tips on opening your own Bakery /Confectionery Outlet:

The main factors driving bakery industry are diverse. This is because the structure of the bakery industry comprises three segments namely need-based, basic hotel requirements and connoisseur requisites. The need-based category caters to products like bread and biscuits. Under hotels, it varies from breads to pastries, cakes, pizza and puffs. The connoisseur category focusses on international standard and will cover products like specialized pastries and cakes.

'Firstly, they should find out what the tastes of the native people are and price the items in accordance to the budget of the people. The bakery unit should be located at a place in the city, which attracts customers. The initial infrastructure may be of low budget and with small space. All is needed in a specialized oven, a marble top table, a mixie and a refrigerator in a small room. If a confectionery has to be set up an air conditioned room is mandatory. 'The products you make depends on the clientele, climate of the place and

what ingredients are easily available. If you open a bakery in a warm country like India you can work with tropical fruits as they are easily available. A good baker should be able to adjust easily. Cream, butter and other ingredients may vary from country to countryrecipes should be adjusted accordingly. A good baker should be able to experiment with flavors.

CHAPTER XVIII

Summary:

In this book we have discussed about various ingredients used in bakery like Sugar, Shortenings, Eggs, Wheat and flours, Milk and milk products, Yeast, Chemical leavening agents, Salt, Spices, Flavorings, Cocoa and Chocolate and Fruits and Nuts. Further we have learnt about Professional bakery equipment and tools, Production Factors and Staling and Spoilage of baked products.

Sugar or as it is chemically called Sucrose is a building blocks of carbohydrates and it is naturally found in many food such as fruit, milk, vegetables and grain, another kind of sugar is added sugar which can be founded in flavored yogurt, sweetened beverages, baked goods and cereals, and it is used widely in industry. Sugar is one of the major ingredients in the bakery industry and plays an important role. Sugars vary in their sweetening quality and are the soul of all desserts. Sugar is natural and non –toxic, sweet testing, water soluble concentrated form or crystalline carbohydrate.

Shortening seems to get its name from the fact that it shortens gluten strands in wheat by adding fat. In other words it is used to prevent the formation of a gluten matrix by interfering with gluten formation in a dough's and batters to impart crisp, flaky and

crumbly texture to baked products such as pie crusts and to increase the plasticity, or workability of dough's. However, some vegetable shortenings have artificial butter flavor added and are used as an inexpensive replacement for butter.

The egg is a biological structure intended by nature for reproduction. It protects and provides a complete diet for the developing embryo, and serves as the principal source of food for the first few days of the chick's life. The egg is also one of the most nutritious and versatile of human foods. The various role that egg plays in baking has been discussed.

Milk most often means the nutrient fluid produced by the mammary glands of female mammals. The female ability to produce milk is one of the defining characteristics of mammals and provides the primary source of nutrition for newborns before they are able to digest more diverse foods.

It is also processed into dairy products such as Cream (food) cream, butter, yogurt, ice- cream, gelato, cheese, casein, whey protein, lactose, condensed milk, powdered milk, and many other food –additive and industrial products. Other than cows and buffalo, milk can also be obtained from sheep, goats, horses, donkeys, camels, yaks, water buffalo and reindeer.

CHAPTER XIX

Glossary:

Agave syrup is produced from starches extracted from. It has a neutral flavor about 25% sweeter than sugar, and a consistency that is thinner than honey. It may be used in baking and cooking, as well as for sweetening beverages.

Brown Sugar – It is simple refined sugar with some molasses returned to it or it is the residual sugar obtained during the process of refining sugar. It is brown in color and has distinctive color and flavor.

Butter – is the fat of milk, separated from milk or cream by churning and contains also a small amount of other milk constituents. Fresh butter consists of about 80% fat, about 15% water, and about 5% milk solids. There are different types of butter available :

Castor sugar – This is superfine sugar (A Grade) and is also called breakfast sugar –made by crushing and sieving fine granulated sugar. It dissolves quickly and easily in liquids and can be creamed easily.

Cell membrane – It is found in the inner lining of the shell. It forms an air cell at the large end, and two white strands called chalazae on the either side hold the yolk at the center of the white.

Chalazae – These thick, twisted strands of egg white anchor the yolk in place. They are neither imperfections nor embryos. The more prominent the chalazae, the fresher the egg. Chalazae do not interfere with cooking or with whipping egg whites.

Clarified butter – It is butter in which water and milk solids have been removed by a process called clarification.

It is although rarely used in bakery only when sometimes a more stable and consistent product is required to be achieved by using clarified butter.

Cleaning: Cleaning begins with screening to remove coarse and fine materials and the grain is separated by size, shape and weight. The finished product, whole pure wheat, is then passed into conditioning bins.

Conditioning: Conditioning takes place before milling to produce uniform moisture content throughout the grain. Moistening helps to prevent break – up of the bran (hard outer layer) during milling and improves separation from the floury endosperm (the mass that forms the white flour of the grain).

Corn Syrup – It is very sweet and contains high amount of fructose and glucose or dextrose. It is chemically refined clear syrup made from corn kernels and is prepared by converting corn starch into simple sugar compound by the use of enzymes.

Date sugar – It is obtained from drying and pulverizing dates. It is very sweet and although it does not dissolve very well it is used in many baked products.

Egg white – It consists $2/3^{rd}$ portion of the egg and is called Albumen. It is clear translucent liquid and contains sulfur and more than half of the albumin protein and riboflavin. The protein, which is clear and soluble when raw but coagulates and becomes firm and opaque at temperatures between 144°F and 149°F (62°C and 65°C) when coagulated.

European –style butter or cultured butter – contains more milk fat than regular butter, usually from 82 to 86 percent with very little or no salt. It is often churned from cultured cream, giving it a more intense, buttery flavor.

Fondant – sugar syrup beaten with cream of tartar to form thick white paste. Used for decorating pastry or confectionary.

Glucose – It is present in body and in fruits in natural form. Commercially it is sold as

Dextrose- It is less sweet than sucrose, but it is use because of its waster holding capacity. It has ability to control the size of the crystals in candies and as a food for yeast, during the fermentation.

Golden Syrups – It is thick amber coloured liquid obtained from sugar during the refining process. It is treated with acid to cut down on the sharp taste. It looks similar to honey and is used in making confectionery products and to add flavour to the food products.

Granulated/ white sugar/sandy sugar –This is the regular white sugar which in used in homes. Usage of this sugar will find its place in any preparation which has sufficient liquid to dissolve it. For example, whipping eggs, making sugar syrups, cooking sabayon over double boilers, etc. It contains 99.7% sucrose.

Gristing: After conditioning, different batches of wheat are blended together (gristed) to make a mix capable of producing the required flour quality.

Heavy syrups – boil equal part of water and sugar for 1 minute. This concentration would measure 28 –30c on the Baume scale, and the solution should be at 220f (104c) heavy syrups are a basic, all – purpose syrup kept on hand in many bakeshops.

Honey –It is natural sugar consisting of glucose and fructose. It is a natural sugar obtained from bee hives. The colour and flavor of honey will vary with its source.

Icing sugar – Granulated sugar is crushed into fine powder and has a small percentage of corn starch added to keep it smooth and free flowing.

Invert sugar –When a sucrose solution is heated with an acid, some of the sucrose breaks down into equal parts of two simple sugars, dextrose and levulose. A mixture of equal parts of dextrose and levulose is called. It is about 30% sweeter than regular sucrose.

Isomalt – It is a natural sugar substitute and in reality it is sugar alcohol. It is available in crystalline forms and is used for preparing sugar garnishes as it is more stable than sugar and does not caramelize thereby giving an appearance of thin glass sheets.

Lactose– It is commercially extracted solution of whey formed by crystallization. It is usually added to bakery products because its presence adds to the brewing of food products.

Lard – is produced from selected fat of the hog through a process known as 'rendering'. It is a solid white product of almost 100 percent pure fat; it contains only a small amount of water.

Light syrups – boil 2 parts water which 1 part sugar for one minute. This concentration would measure – 17 –20c on the Baume scale. Light syrups can be used for making sorbet or moistening sponge cake.

Liquid caramel – liquid sugar in which caramel colour is added to give it dark brown colour. It is a thick free –flowing liquid and may be used in preparation of puddings and some types of confectionary.

Liquid glucose – Liquid glucose is obtained by treating the corn slurry by acid – a process known as hydrolysis.

Maltose – It is use as a flavoring and coloring agent in the brewing of beer.

Maple syrup – It is natural sweetener and is a sap of maple tree. It is boiled down to thick syrup. Pure maple syrup is very expensive, as to obtain 1 liter of maple one has to boil down at least 10 liters of maple sap. For easy processing, commercial maple syrup added to them. It could be added in the range of 2 –6 percent. The percentage of the maple is always mentioned on the bottle and this decides the price of the product.

Medium syrup – boil 1 part sugar with 1 – ½ part water for 1 minute. This concentration would measure 21 –24c on the Baume scale. Medium syrups can be used for candying citrus peel.

Muscovado sugar – is an unrefined or partially refined cane sugar with a strong molasses flavor and high moisture content. It has a slightly coarse texture and feels sticky to the touch. It is popularly used in chocolate sweets and other baked goods. It is also called Barbados sugar, molasses sugar, kandasari, khand, and moist sugar.

Palm sugar – Palm sugar is traditionally made from the sap of Palmyra palm or the date palm. It is extensively used in Asian cooking.

Pearl sugar – is a type of decorating sugar made by polishing large crystals until they resemble pearls.

Powder Sugar or confectioners' sugar – It is obtained from granulated sugar by pulverization (refining of granulated sugar to get more fine form). It is available in various degree of fineness, use for different purposes in confectionary.

Salted butter – It is butter with up to 2.5 percent salt added, which not only changes the butter's flavor, it also extends its keeping qualities. When salted butter is used, the salt content must be considered in the total recipe.

Sugar cubes – are formed by pressing moistened granulated sugar into molds and allowing it to dry. Most cubes are used for beverage service.

The shell – The shell, composed of calcium carbonateis not only fragile but also porous, is the outermost covering of the egg. It prevents microbes from entering and moisture from escaping, and also protects the egg during handling and transport. The breed of the hen determines shell color; for chickens, it can range from bright white to brown. Shell color has no effect on quality, flavor or nutrition.

The Yolk – It is the yellow portion of the egg. It constitutes just over one –third of the egg and contains three –fourths of the calories, most of the minerals and vitamins and all the fat. The yolk also contains lecithin, the compound responsible for emulsification in products such as hollandaise sauce and mayonnaise. Egg yolk solidifies (coagulates) at temperatures between 149°F and 158°F (65°C and 70°C). Although the color of a yolk may vary depending on the hen's feed, color does not affect quality or nutritional content.

Treacle/Molasses – are products of refined sugar. When the sugarcane juice undergoes refining, it undergoes many stages. In the first stage the white sugar or the raw sugar is removed. The remaining sugar syrup is used to make treacle which is stronger than golden syrup but less than molasses. Used in the preparation of certain beverages and sauces.

Unsalted butter – It is more perishable, but it has a fresher, sweeter taste and is thus preferred in baking.

Vergeoise sugar or Sucre vergeoise (French) – solid residue from refining beet giving a product of soft consistency, golden or brown with pronounced color.v Sucre vergeoise is available in blonde (light) or brune (dark).

Whipped butter – It is made by incorporating air into the butter. This increases its volume and spreadability but also increases the speed with which the butter will become rancid. Because of the change in density, whipped butter should not be substituted in recipes calling for regular butter.

The Author

Dr. Anshumali Pandey, is a renowned & reliable name in the field of Education, Hospitality, Tourism and Tribal Food. He is a Teacher and Chef by profession, and also an Author, a Business Auditor, and an avid culinary traveller to the Indian Sub continental hinterlands. Dr. Anshumali Pandey is a Hospitality Educator (PhD) who specialises in Higher Education, Office Administration, Pay roll, HR, Labour Laws, Audit, and Procurement & Tender Process. He is an Author with 48 Publications consisting of 33 Books.

The books written by Dr Anshumali Pandey are essentially a banquet arising from an experience of over 25 years of Professional life and have boiled down to crisp and accurate writing on his favourite subjects. Hospitality Sector champion requires to be a specialist in many fields and Dr Pandey is one of them. His knowledge is evident from the spectrum of subjects which he has chosen for his books so far, which ranges from being a specialist chef, to Master of Human resources, to Education and to love for children, and topped with Spirituality.

Books written by the Author are –

1. Theory of Indian Cookery
2. Beauty and Irony of Silvassa Tourism
3. A Short Indian Food Story
4. Be Your Own Guide to Indian Cuisine
5. Cookery Fundamentals
6. History of Indian Food
7. The Great Indian Story Book for Children
8. Personal Budget: Easy Work Book

9. Online Classes Log Book
10. Dictionary Making Work Book for School Children
11. The Lazy Bed
12. Hindu Dharm (हिन्दू धर्म) (In Hindi Language)
13. Where is my coffee?
14. Your First Job is Never your Last (Volume 1)
15. You are Almost There (Quick Fix Resume and Interview Hacks)
16. Working for the Enemy? - A lesson in Career Management
17. Public Speaking for the Young
18. A Date With Coffee
19. How to be The Best Hotel Front Office Employee
20. Diploma in Food Production, The complete Syllabus
21. Diploma in F&B Service, The Complete Syllabus
22. Diploma in Front Office, The Complete Syllabus
23. The Time to Speak is Now
24. Munshi Premchand (Short Stories in English)
25. The Housekeeping Department, Text Book
26. Hitchhiker's Guide to Trekking in Uttarakhand
27. Uttarakhand, A divine Land for a Reason
28. Bachhon ke liye rochak kahaniyan (बच्चों के लिए रोचक कहानियाँ) (In Hindi Language)
29. Basic Communication Skills of English
30. The Basic Office Organisation Book for Start-ups
31. Hospitality HRM
32. Hospitality Marketing
33. Bakery Ingredients and Tools

Connect with me: anshumali.pandey@gmail.com
https://notionpress.com/author/337004

DR ANSHUMALI PANDEY, PHD, AUTHOR.

Please scan this QR Code for information about the Author and his latest books.

9 798887 045122

Printed by Libri Plureos GmbH in Hamburg, Germany